Microsoft® Excel

SIMPLY° VISUAL

Microsoft® Excel

SIMPLY VISUAL™

Perspection, Inc.

SYBEX®

San Francisco ◆ Paris ◆ Düsseldorf ◆ Soest ◆ London

Associate Publisher: Cheryl Applewood
Contracts and Licensing Manager: Kristine O'Callaghan
Acquisitions & Development Editor: Bonnie Bills
Managing Editor: Steve Johnson
Author: Elizabeth Eisner Reding
Editor: Barbara Waxer
Production Editor: Marian Hartsough
Technical Editors: Tracy Teyler and Kristy Thielen
Book Designer: Maureen Forys, Happenstance Type-O-Rama
Electronic Publishing Specialist: Marian Hartsough
Proofreaders: Beth Teyler and Shirley Todd
Indexer: Michael Brackney
Cover Designer: Daniel Ziegler
Cover Illustrator: Ziegler Design

Library of Congress Card Number: 2001090113

ISBN: 0-7821-4006-8

Manufactured in the United States of America

10 9 8 7 6 5 4 3 2 1

···

To my wife,
the Excel queen
and the mother of
JP, Brett, and Hannah.
Steve

Perspection

Perspection, Inc., is a software training company committed to providing information and training to help people use software more effectively in order to communicate, make decisions, and solve problems. Perspection writes and produces software training books, and develops multimedia and Web-based training. This incorporates Perspection's training expertise to ensure that you'll receive the maximum return on your time. With this straightforward, easy-to-read reference tool, you get the information you need to get the job done.

We invite you to visit the Perspection Web site at:

www.perspection.com

Acknowledgments

The task of creating any book requires the talents of many hardworking people pulling together to meet almost impossible demands. For their effort and commitment, we'd like to thank the outstanding team responsible for making this book possible: the writer, Elizabeth Eisner Reding; the editor, Barbara Waxer; the technical editors, Tracy Teyler and Kristy Thielen; the production editor, Marian Hartsough; the proofreaders, Beth Teyler and Shirley Todd; and the indexer, Michael Brackney.

At Sybex, we'd like to thank Jordan Gold and Cheryl Applewood for the opportunity to undertake this project, Bonnie Bills for her editorial support, and Amy Changar, Judith Hibbard, and Cheryl Hauser for their direction and guidance with the printing process.

Perspection

Contents

Contents

Contents

Introduction

This book offers a simple visual approach to learning Microsoft Excel 2002. Designed for the beginner who may find the complexity of the Excel program intimidating, *Microsoft Excel 2002 Simply Visual* uses a highly visual, step-by-step format to present the fundamental tasks that any new user needs in order to get "up and running" as quickly as possible on the Excel 2002 program that is the industry standard.

How This Book Is Organized

Microsoft Excel 2002 Simply Visual is designed to be an easy-to-read and easy-to-use reference tool that helps you get your work done quickly and efficiently in a straightforward way. Each chapter is organized by tasks. Each task gives you information that is essential to performing the task. For each operation, you'll see what commands to enter and which options to select.

This book contains thirteen chapters. In Chapter 1, you'll learn the essentials for getting started with Excel 2002. Chapter 2 covers the basic workbook skills you need to enter data and check your work. Chapter 3 covers tasks for creating and using formulas and functions in a worksheet. Chapters 4 and 5 cover tasks for modifying and formatting worksheets and workbooks. Chapter 6 covers tasks for inserting and modifying graphics, stylized text, organization charts, and diagrams. Chapter 7 covers tasks for drawing and modifying shapes and objects. Chapter 8 covers tasks for creating and modifying charts using data from a worksheet. Chapter 9 covers tasks for analyzing worksheet data. Chapter 10 and 11 cover tasks for sharing workbooks and collaborating with others. Chapter 12 covers tasks for creating Web pages from a workbook and working on the Web from Excel. Chapter 13 covers tasks for customizing Excel to the way you work.

How to Make Good Use of This Book

We recommend using this book as a kind of beginner's reference. Use the index or table of contents to find the command or feature you want to learn about and go directly there. Each basic operation is presented as a step-by-step procedure, with illustrations to guide you. Simple but realistic examples allow you to try out most procedures on your own. As key terms are introduced, you'll find capsule definitions in the margin. (These definitions are also gathered into a Glossary at the end of the book, so you can look up a term at any time.) Margin notes also provide alternative methods to accomplish particular steps and summarize important concepts.

Every reader should begin with the first chapter, especially if you are not at all familiar with Excel 2002. After that, you can jump to any of the chapters that meet your needs. Keep the book near your workstation for quick access as you work on your projects. If a command or procedure confuses you, you can easily flip to the two or three pages that describe it.

We hope this book serves you as a useful guide as you learn and use Excel 2002.

1 Getting Started with Excel

Excel is a spreadsheet program that you can use to track and analyze sales, create budgets, and organize finances—both business and personal. You can use Excel to perform calculations and other tasks automatically, which allows you to accomplish a variety of business tasks in a fraction of the time it would take using pen and paper. This chapter introduces you to the terminology and the basic Excel skills you will use in the program. In Excel, files are called **workbooks**. Each new workbook contains three **worksheets**, which are similar to the pages in an accountant's ledger. You perform calculations and other tasks in the worksheets.

Starting Excel

Before you can begin using Excel, you need to start the program. The easiest way to start Excel is to use the Start menu, which you open by clicking the Start button on the taskbar. When Excel starts, it displays a new **workbook** and three **worksheets** so that you can begin working immediately in the **spreadsheet program**.

Start Excel from the Start Menu

Workbook
The file you create that contains one or more worksheets.

Worksheet
A page from a workbook that contains lines and grids.

Spreadsheet program
A type of software you can use to enter, evaluate, manipulate, and communicate quantitative information.

1. Click the **Start** button 🔣**Start** on the taskbar.

2. Point to **Programs**.

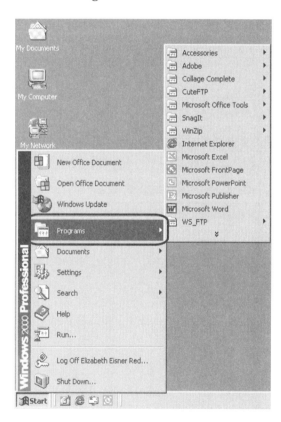

Task pane
An expanded display area to the right of the main window that displays groups of related commands and wizards.

3. Click **Microsoft Excel**. A blank workbook opens, and the New Workbook **task pane** opens on the right side of the screen.

Viewing the Excel Window

When Excel opens, the program window displays a blank workbook—ready for you to begin working.

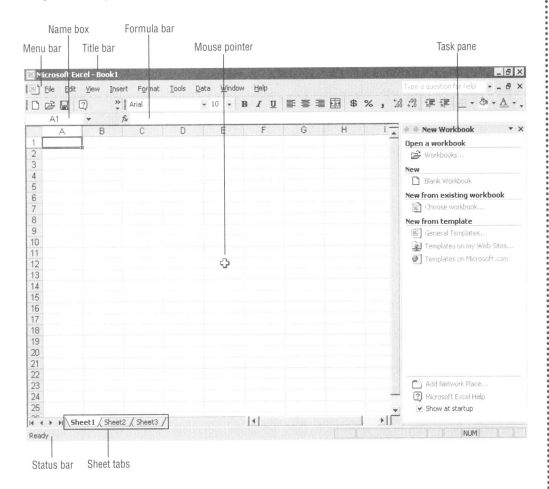

You can open more than one workbook window at a time. That means that if you are working with one workbook and need to check or work with data in another, you don't need to close the current file. You can view open windows one at a time, or arrange all of them on the screen at the same time, and then click the window in which you want to work. You can also move and resize each window to suit your viewing needs and work habits.

TIP You can easily navigate from Excel to documents open in other programs. Each open document displays its own button on the Windows taskbar. You can switch between the open files by clicking the icons on the taskbar or by holding down the Alt+Tab keys on the keyboard.

Switch Between Workbook Windows

1. Click the **Window** menu to display the list of open workbook windows.

2. Click the name of the workbook to which you want to switch.

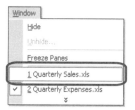

Resize and Move Windows

You can change the size and position of a workbook using buttons in the upper-right corner of its window.

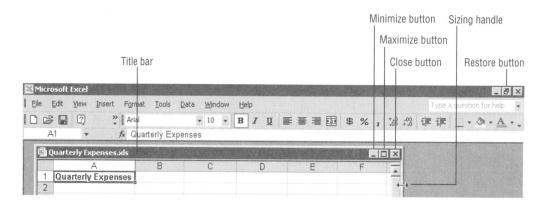

Minimize a window To reduce a window to an icon on the taskbar, click the **Minimize** button .

Maximize a window To maximize a window to fit the screen, click the **Maximize** button .

Resize a window To change the size of the window, position the mouse pointer over any edge of the window, and then click and drag the sizing handle to the size you want.

Move a window To change a window's location on your screen, drag the title bar of the workbook window to a different spot.

Starting a New Workbook

When you start Excel, the program window opens with a new workbook so that you can begin working in it. You can also start a new workbook whenever Excel is running, and you can start as many new workbooks as you want. Each new workbook displays a default name and is numbered consecutively during the current work session (Book1, Book2, and so on). When you save a workbook with a unique name, Excel's numbering scheme for the next workbook restarts from the last assigned number. Each time you start a work session, the numbering scheme restarts from "1."

Start a New Workbook from the Task Pane

1. Click the **File** menu, and then click the **New** command (**File ➤ New**).

2. Click **Blank Workbook**. Excel opens a blank workbook.

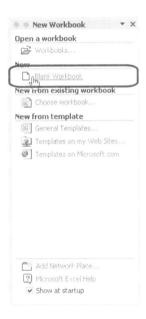

Start a New Workbook from the New Button

1. Click the **New** button ⬜. Excel opens a blank workbook.

Opening an Existing Workbook

When you want to use a workbook you have previously created, you must first open it. You can open an Excel workbook and start Excel simultaneously, or you can open an Excel workbook file (or a file created in another spreadsheet program) after you start Excel. If you can't remember the workbook's name or location, Excel even helps you find the files.

NOTE   Excel saves files to a default location on your hard drive or on a network drive unless you change the default settings. To change the default file location of where Excel opens files, choose Tools ➢ Options, click the General tab, and then enter a new location in the Default File Location box.

Open a Workbook from the Excel Window

1. Click the **Open** button 📂 on the Standard toolbar. The Open dialog box opens.

2. Click one of the icons on the **Places** bar for quick access to frequently used folders.

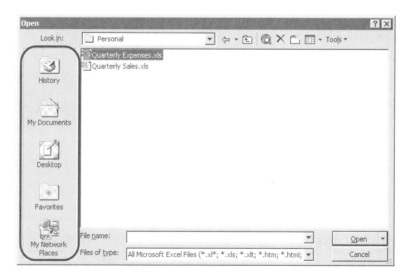

3. If the file is located in another folder, click the **Look In** drop-down arrow ▾, and select the drive or folder containing the file you want to open.

4. If you want to open a different type of Excel file or other files, click the **Files Of Type** drop-down arrow ▾, and then click the type of file you want to open (click **Microsoft Excel Files** to see workbook files).

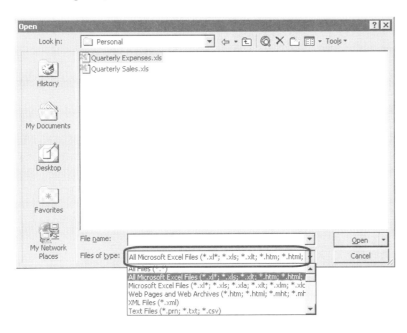

5. Click the name of the workbook file you want to open.

6. Click the **Open** button.

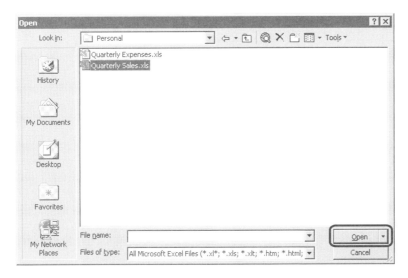

NOTE Can't find a file created in another spreadsheet program? If the name of the spreadsheet program you want to open doesn't appear in the Files Of Type list, use the Excel setup program to install the necessary filters.

TIP If you have recently opened and closed a workbook, you can reopen it by clicking the file-name at the bottom of the File menu. You can increase or decrease the number of recently opened files that appear on the File menu. Choose Tools ➤ Options, click the General tab, and then change the number in the Recently Used File List box.

Open a Recently Opened Workbook from the Start Menu

1. Click the **Start** button 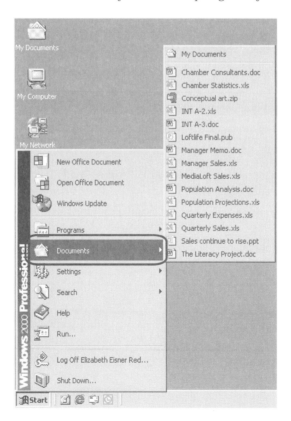 on the taskbar.

2. Point to **Documents**. The Documents menu displays a list of documents from every Windows program you've recently opened.

3. Click the Excel workbook that you want to open.

Navigating a Worksheet

You can move around a worksheet or workbook using your mouse or the keyboard. You might find that using your mouse is most convenient when moving from cell to cell, while using various keyboard combinations is easier for covering large areas of a worksheet quickly. However, there is no one right way; whichever method feels the most comfortable is the one you should use. You can also use the arrow keys on the keyboard, but bear in mind if you are moving across several cells, arrow keys are less effective and can cause eyestrain.

> **TIP**   Microsoft IntelliMouse users can roll from cell to cell with IntelliMouse. If you have the new Microsoft IntelliMouse—with the wheel button between the left and right buttons—you can click the wheel button and move the mouse in any direction to move quickly around the worksheet.

Use the Mouse to Navigate

Using the mouse, you can navigate to one of the following:

- ◇ Another cell
- ◇ Another part of a worksheet
- ◇ Another worksheet

> **TIP**   Instead of scrolling when you roll with the IntelliMouse, you can zoom in or out. To turn on this feature, choose Tools ➣ Options, click the General tab, click the Zoom On Roll With IntelliMouse check box to select it, and then click the OK button.

Use the Keyboard to Navigate

Using the keyboard, you can navigate to one of the following:

- ✪ Another cell
- ✪ Another part of a worksheet

Refer to the table for keyboard shortcuts for navigating around a worksheet.

Press This Key	To Move
Left arrow	One cell to the left
Right arrow	One cell to the right
Up arrow	One cell up
Down arrow	One cell down
Enter	One cell down
Tab	One cell to the right
Shift+Tab	One cell to the left
Page Up	One screen up
Page Down	One screen down
End+arrow	In the direction of the arrow key to the next cell that contains data or to the last empty cell in the current row or column
Home	To column A in the current row
Ctrl+Home	To cell A1
Ctrl+End	To the last cell in the worksheet that contains data

TIP When you press the Enter key on the keyboard, Excel's default is to move the active cell down one cell. To change the default direction, choose Tools ➤ Options, click the Edit tab, click the Direction drop-down arrow, select a direction, and then click the OK button.

Choosing Commands

All Excel commands are organized on menus on the menu bar. Under each menu, you will find a list of commands related to the menu category. A short menu displays commonly used commands, and an expanded menu displays all of the remaining commands available on that menu. A menu command followed by an ellipsis (...) indicates that a **dialog box** opens, which is where you can provide additional information for the command. An arrow to the right of a command indicates that a submenu contains additional choices and related commands. An icon to the left of the command indicates that a toolbar button is available for that command. Toolbars contain buttons that you can click to perform the commands that you use most often. A keyboard combination to the right of a menu command indicates that a shortcut key or combination of keys on the keyboard is available for the command.

Dialog box
A window that displays onscreen that you use to enter or select information.

Choose a Command Using a Menu

1. Click a menu name on the menu bar to display a list of commands.

2. If necessary, click the double-headed arrow to expand the menu and display more commands, or wait a few seconds until the expanded list of commands appears.

3. Choose the command you want in the menu, or if a submenu is available, point to the arrow to the right of the menu command and then click a command.

11

Choose a Command Using a Toolbar Button

1. If you're not sure what a toolbar button does, move the mouse over a button to display a ScreenTip.

2. To choose a command, click the button on the toolbar. If the button you want is not displayed, click the **Toolbar Options** drop-down arrow 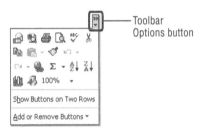, and then click the button.

The commands and buttons that appear on menus and toolbars respond to your work habits. Certain commands and buttons appear by default. As you select other menu commands or toolbar buttons, Excel promotes them to the short menu and shared toolbar.

Toolbar Options button

TIP You can customize toolbars to your preference by moving and reshaping them. A toolbar that appears at the top or on the edge of a window is docked; if it appears somewhere else on the screen, it is floating. To move a toolbar to another location, click a blank area of the toolbar (not a button), and then drag the toolbar to a new location. To change the shape of a floating toolbar, position the mouse pointer over the edge of the toolbar, and then drag the border to reshape it.

Select Dialog Box and Wizard Options

A dialog box is a special window that opens when Excel needs additional information from you in order to complete a task. You indicate your choices by selecting a variety of option buttons and check boxes; in some cases, you type the necessary information in the boxes provided. Some dialog boxes consist of a single window, while others contain tabs that you click to display more sets of options. **Wizards** are special dialog boxes that guide you through a task; they are powerful tools that make complicated tasks easy, such as creating a chart or analyzing data.

A dialog box may contain several components that require your input. After you select the options you want or enter the necessary information, you can perform one of two options, listed below.

◇ Click the **OK** button to complete the command and close the dialog box.

◇ Click the **Cancel** button or press the Esc key on the keyboard to cancel the command and any information you selected, and close the dialog box.

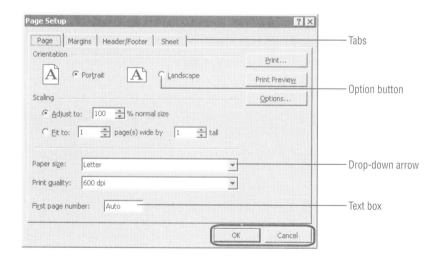

Getting Help

Excel provides an extensive Help system to guide you in completing tasks. You can get help any time in Excel using the Help menu, the Ask a Question box, or the **Office Assistant**, which in addition to answering questions, can automatically

Wizard
A utility that leads you through steps to produce a product or accomplish a task.

Office Assistant
An animated Help feature that displays helpful tips while you are working in Excel.

ScreenTip

Descriptive text hat displays when you hold the pointer over a button.

provide advice on Excel features as you work. You can ask the Office Assistant how to accomplish a task or to learn helpful information about Excel functions. **ScreenTips** show toolbar names and short descriptions about anything you see on the screen or in a dialog box, and arguments in a function in a cell.

> **TIP** You can open the Office Assistant by clicking the Help button. If the Office Assistant is already turned on, you will see the Office Assistant at the top of your screen.

Show or Hide the Office Assistant

1. Click the **Help** menu to open it.

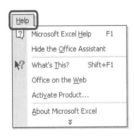

2. Click **Show The Office Assistant** to turn it on, or click **Hide The Office Assistant** to turn it off.

> **NOTE** You can turn off the Office Assistant by using the shortcut menu. Simply right-click the Office Assistant, click Options, click the Use The Office Assistant check box to clear it, and then click the OK button.

Ask for Help from the Office Assistant

1. Click the **Office Assistant** or click the **Help** button on the Standard toolbar.

2. Type your question (it does not have to be in the form of a question).

3. Click the **Search** button.

4. Click the button for the topic in which you're interested.

5. Read the topic, view a demonstration, or click a hyperlink to another topic.

6. Click the **Close** button ⊠.

TIP   The Office Assistant provides interactive help. If you see a Show Me link in Help, click the link to display a demonstration of how to perform the task.

Get a ScreenTip

1. Place the mouse pointer over a toolbar button. The name of the button, or the ScreenTip, appears below the button. If you are in a dialog box, right-click an item, and then click What' This? to display a description.

TIP To hide ScreenTips, choose Tools ➤ Customize, click the Options tab, click the Show ScreenTips On check box to clear it, and then click the OK button.

TIP You can display ScreenTips for function arguments. Click a cell, type a function, and a screen tip appears showing all of the arguments for the function. The ScreenTip also provides a link to the Help topic for the function.

Get Help While You Work

1. Click the Ask a Question box 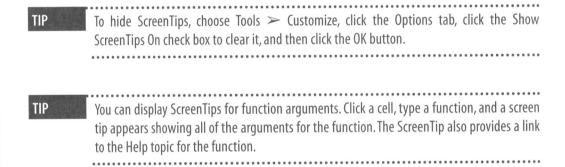 on the right-side of the menu bar.

2. Type a question, and then press the Enter key.

3. Click a topic on the menu. The Microsoft Excel Help window opens.

Saving a Workbook

When you create a new Excel workbook, the title bar displays a default title, such as Book1 or Book2. When you save a workbook for the first time, you need to give it a meaningful name and specify where you want to store it. Once you have saved a workbook, you should save it before you close the file so that you save the changes you've made during that work session. If you have opened an existing file and want to change it but also preserve the original version, just save the modified workbook with a different name. Now you have the original workbook and the workbook to which you've made changes. If necessary, you can also change the file format so that you can use the workbook file with a different program.

Save a Workbook for the First Time

1. Click the **Save** button 🖫 on the Standard toolbar. The Save As dialog box opens.

2. Click one of the icons on the **Places** bar (quick access to frequently used folders) to select the location where you will save the workbook file. The default folder is **My Documents**.

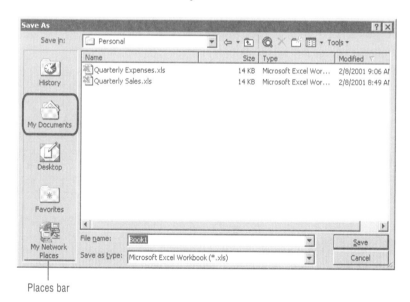

Places bar

3. If you want to save the file in another folder, click the **Save In** drop-down arrow ![arrow], and then select the drive and folder in which you want to store the workbook file.

4. In the **File Name** box, type the file name for the new workbook name.

5. Click the **Save** button. The new name appears in the title bar of the workbook.

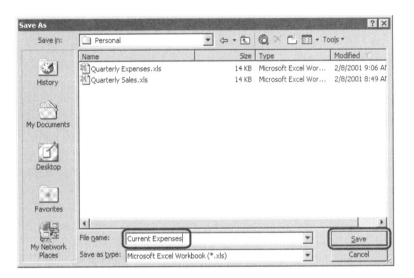

NOTE You can save a workbook you created in Excel 2002 for a user of an earlier version of Excel. From the Save As dialog box, click the Save As Type drop-down arrow, and then select a previous version of Excel from the list.

TIP You can create a new folder in the Save As and Open dialog boxes. In the Save As or Open dialog box, click the Create New Folder button, type the name of the folder in the Name box, and then click the OK button.

Save an Existing Workbook with a Different Name and in a Different Format

1. Choose **File ➤ Save As**. The Save As dialog box opens.

2. Click one of the icons on the **Places** bar for quick access to frequently used folders.

3. If you want to save the file in another folder, click the **Save In** drop-down arrow ![arrow], and then select the drive and folder in which you want to save the workbook file.

4. In the **File Name** box, type the new file name.

5. Click the **Save As Type** drop-down arrow ![arrow].

6. Select the file format you want.

7. Click the **Save** button.

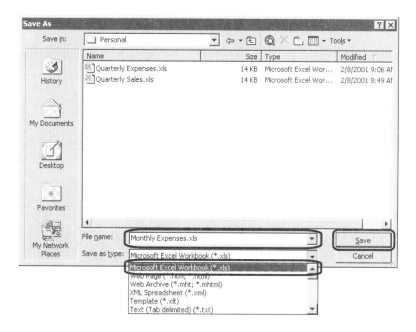

Recovering a Document

If an Office program encounters a problem and stops responding, the program tries to recover the document the next time you open the program. The recovered documents appear in the Document Recovery task pane, which allows you to open the files, view what repairs were made, and compare the recovered versions. Each file appears in the task pane with a status indicator, either Original or Recovered, which shows what type of data recovery was performed. You can save one or all of the document versions. For each file you want to keep, point to the file in the Document Recovery task pane, click the down arrow, and then click Open or Save As. You can also use the AutoRecover feature to periodically save a temporary copy of your current file, which ensures proper recovery of the file. To turn on AutoRecover feature, choose Tools ➤ Options, click the Save tab, click the Save AutoRecover Info Every check box, type a number of minutes in the box, and then click the OK button.

Previewing and Printing a Worksheet

You should always preview your work before sending it to the printer. By using **print preview**, you can view all or part of your worksheet as it will appear when you print it. You can print a copy of your worksheet by clicking the Print button on the Standard toolbar or on the Print Preview toolbar. You can open the Print dialog box to specify several print options, such as choosing a new printer, selecting the number of pages in the worksheet you want printed, and specifying the number of copies.

Preview a Worksheet

1. Click the **Print Preview** button 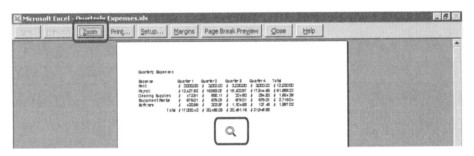 on the Standard toolbar, or choose **File ➤ Print Preview**.

2. Click the **Zoom** button on the Print Preview toolbar, or position the Zoom pointer anywhere on the worksheet and click it to enlarge a specific area of the page.

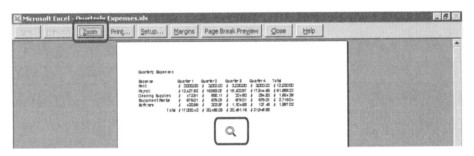

3. If you do not want to print from Print Preview, click the **Close** button to return to the worksheet.

4. If you want to print from Print Preview, click the **Print** button on the Print Preview toolbar to open the Print dialog box.

5. From the Print dialog box, specify the printing options you want, and then click the **OK** button, or click the **Preview** button to return to Print Preview.

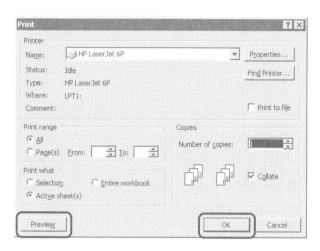

Print a Copy of a Worksheet Quickly

1. Click the **Print** button 🖨 on the Standard toolbar. Excel prints the selected worksheet with the current Print dialog box settings.

TIP To change printer properties, choose File ➤ Print, and then click Properties to change general printer properties for paper size and orientation, graphics, and fonts.

TIP When you select the Collate check box, Excel prints multiple copies of a worksheet in complete sets. For two copies of a two-page document, the Collate option prints pages 1 and 2, and then prints pages 1 and 2 again.

Specify Print Options Using the Print Dialog Box

1. Choose **File** ➢ **Print**. The Print dialog box opens.

2. To choose another (installed) printer, click the **Name** drop-down arrow ▾, and then select the printer you want to use from the list.

3. To print selected pages (rather than all pages), click the **Page(s)** option button, and then click the **From** and **To** up or down arrows to specify the page range you want.

4. To print more than one copy of the print range, click the **Number Of Copies** up or down arrow to specify the number of copies you want.

5. To change the worksheet print area, click one of the **Print What** option buttons that correctly identifies the area to be printed.

6. Click the **OK** button.

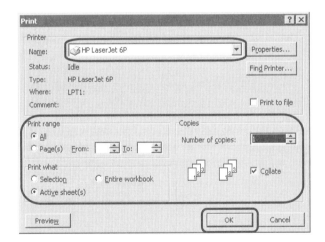

Exiting Excel

After you finish working on a workbook, you can close it and open another workbook, or close it and quit Excel. Closing a workbook makes more computer memory available for other processes. Closing a workbook is different from quitting Excel: after you close a workbook, Excel is still running. When you're finished using Excel, you can quit the program. To protect your files, always quit Excel before turning off your computer.

Close a Workbook

1. Choose **File ➤ Close**, or click the **Close** button ⊠ on the worksheet window title bar. If you have made any changes to the workbook since last saving it, the Office Assistant asks if you want to save the workbook.

2. Click the **Yes** button to save any workbook changes; click the **No** button to close the workbook without saving any changes; or click the **Cancel** button to return to the workbook without closing it.

Quit Excel

1. Choose **File** ➢ **Exit**, or click the **Close** button on the Excel program window title bar.

> **NOTE** When you close a file that you've modified but have not yet saved, a dialog box opens asking if you want to save your changes.

2. Click the **Yes** button to save any workbook changes, or click the **No** button to ignore any changes.

2 Basic Workbook Skills

Creating a Microsoft Excel workbook is as simple as entering data in the cells of an Excel worksheet. Cells contain labels, values, or a combination of both. You can modify entries using the keyboard or mouse. In addition, you can use several Excel tools to simplify data entry and correct spelling errors. Another feature allows you to move or copy the contents of one or more cells into other cells, which increases your efficiency and decreases the amount of time you spend typing.

Making Label Entries

Excel has three types of cell entries: labels, values, and formulas. Excel uses values and formulas to perform its calculations. A **label** is text in a cell that identifies the data on the worksheet so readers can interpret the information, such as titles or column headings. A **value** is a number you enter in a cell. To enter values easily and quickly, you can format a cell, a range of cells, or an entire column with a specific number-related format.

To perform a calculation in a worksheet, you enter a formula in a cell. A **formula** performs an operation on one or more cells. Excel calculates the formula based on cell references, values, and arithmetic operators. The result of a formula appears in the worksheet cell where you entered the formula. When you enter a formula in a cell, the contents appear on the formula bar. Entering cell references rather than actual values in a formula has distinct advantages. When you change the data in the worksheet (for example, changing the contents of cell C4 from .45 to .55) or copy the formula to other cells (copying a formula to the cell below), Excel automatically adjusts the cell references in the formula and returns the correct results.

Select a Contiguous Range

In order to work with a cell—to enter data in it, edit or move it, or perform an action—you **select** the cell so it becomes the active cell. When you want to work with more than one cell at a time—to move or copy them, use them in a formula, or perform any group action—you must first select the cells as a **range**. A range can be **contiguous** (where selected cells are adjacent to each other) or **noncontiguous** (where the cells may be in different parts of the worksheet and are not adjacent to each other). As you select a range, you can see the range reference in the Name box. A **range reference** contains the cell

---

Label
Cell text used in titles and column or row headings, and not included in calculations.

Value
The number you enter in a cell that is in calculations.

Formula
A series of values, cell references, and mathematical operators that results in a calculation.

Select
Click a cell to make it active.

Range
One or more cells that you've selected.

Contiguous
Adjacent, or touching, cells.

Noncontiguous
Cells that are not adjacent, or touching.

Range reference
The cell address that displays in the name box.

address of the top-left cell in the range, a colon (:), and the cell address of the bottom-right cell in the range.

> **TIP** To deselect a range, click anywhere in the worksheet.

1. Click the first cell you want to include in the range.

2. Drag the mouse to the last cell you want to include in the range. When you select a range, the cell pointer surrounds the top-left cell, and Excel highlights the additional cells in color.

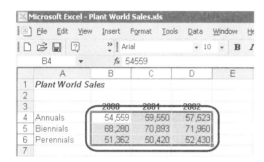

Select a Noncontiguous Range

1. Click the first cell you want to include in the range.

2. Drag the mouse to the last contiguous cell, and then release the mouse button.

3. Hold down the Ctrl key on the keyboard, and then click the next cell, or drag the mouse pointer over the next group of cells you want in the range.

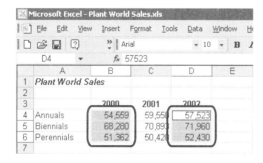

4. Repeat step 3 until you select the cells you want.

Enter a Text Label

AutoComplete

A feature that finishes entering your text entries based on the entries you previously entered in a column. AutoComplete does not work with numbers, dates, or times.

Labels turn a worksheet full of numbers into a meaningful report by identifying the different types of information it contains. You use labels to describe or identify the data in worksheet cells, columns, and rows. You can enter a number as a label (for example, the year 2002), so that Excel does not use the number in its calculations. To help keep your labels consistent, you can use Excel's **AutoComplete** feature, which automatically completes your entries based on the format of previously entered labels.

TIP You can accept an entry in different ways. After you've entered a value, you can click the Enter button on the formula bar to leave the insertion point in the active cell, or you can press the Enter key on the keyboard to move the insertion point down one cell on the worksheet.

1. Click the cell where you want to enter a label.

2. Type a label. A label can include uppercase and lowercase letters, spaces, punctuation, and numbers.

3. Press the Enter key on the keyboard, or click the **Enter** button ☑ on the formula bar.

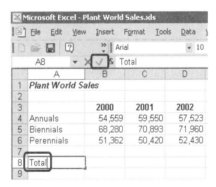

Enter a Number as a Label

1. Click the cell where you want to enter a number as a label.

2. Type ' (an apostrophe). The apostrophe is a label prefix and does not appear on the worksheet—it instructs Excel to treat the contents as text, not as a value.

3. Type a number. Examples of numbers that you might use as labels include a year, a tax form number, or a part number.

4. Press the Enter key on the keyboard, or click the **Enter** button 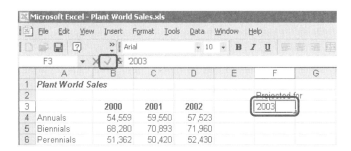 on the formula bar.

NOTE ⬝⬝⬝
When you enter a label that is wider than the cell it occupies, the excess text appears to spill into the next cell to the right—unless there is data in the adjacent cell. If that cell contains data, the label will appear truncated—you'll only see the portion of the label that fits in the cell's current width. Click the cell to see its entire contents displayed on the formula bar.
⬝⬝⬝

Enter a Label Using AutoComplete

1. Type the first few characters of a label. If Excel recognizes the entry, AutoComplete completes it.

2. To accept the suggested entry, press the Enter key on the keyboard or click the **Enter** button on the formula bar.

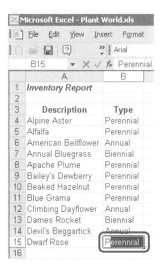

If you receive an error that Excel does not recognize the entry, verify that the AutoComplete option is turned on. To turn on the feature, click Tools ➢ Options, and then click the Edit tab, click the Enable AutoComplete For Cell Values check box to select it, and then click the OK button.

3. To reject the suggested completion, simply continue typing.

Entering Values

You can enter values as whole numbers, decimals, percentages, or dates. You can enter values using the numbers on the top row of your keyboard, or the numeric keypad on the right side of your keyboard. When you enter a date or the time of day, Excel automatically recognizes these entries (if entered in an acceptable format) as numeric values and changes the cell's format to a default date, currency, or time format.

> **NOTE** You can use the numeric keypad like a calculator to enter numbers on your worksheet. Before using the numeric keypad, make sure NUM appears in the lower-right corner of the status bar. If NUM is not displayed, you can turn on this feature by pressing the Num Lock key on the numeric keypad.

Enter a Value

1. Click the cell where you want to enter a value.

2. Type a value. To simplify your data entry, type the values without commas and dollar signs. You can apply a numeric format to them later.

3. Press the Enter key on the keyboard, or click the **Enter** button 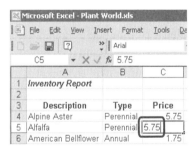 on the formula bar.

Enter a Date or Time

1. To enter a date, type the date using a slash (/) or a hyphen (-) between the month, day, and year in a cell or on the formula bar. You can enter single months or days as one numeral.

To enter a time, type the hour based on a 12-hour clock, followed by a colon (:), followed by the minute, followed by a space, and ending with an "A" or a "P" to denote AM. or PM.

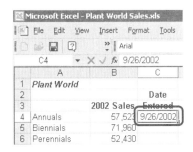

2. Press the Enter key on the keyboard, or click the **Enter** button ☑ on the formula bar.

Change Date or Time Format

1. Click the cell that contains the date format you want to change.

2. Choose **Format** ➤ **Cells**. The Format Cells dialog box opens.

3. Click the **Number** tab.

4. In the **Category** list, click **Date**.

5. Click the date or time format you want from the **Type** list.

6. Click the **OK** button.

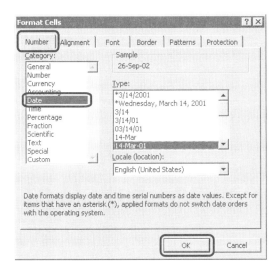

You can shorten data entry time by applying a cell format to a cell. When you enter a value, you don't have to type additional formatting characters, such as periods or decimal places. For example, to enter the value "10.00", simply type "10." Choose Format ➤ Cells to format your cell entries with other formatting attributes such as commas, currency symbols, negative numbers, zip code + 4, or dates.

Enter Repeating Data Using AutoFill

The **AutoFill** feature automatically fills in data based on the data in adjacent cells. Using the **fill handle**, you can enter data in a series, or you can copy values or formulas to adjacent cells. The entry in a cell can create an AutoFill that repeats a value or label, or the results can be a more complex extended series, such as days of the week, months of the year, or consecutive numbering.

After you fill text or data in a worksheet, the AutoFill Options button appears. You can click the AutoFill button to display additional options, such as Copy Cells, Fill Series, Fill Formatting Only, or Fill Without Formatting.

> **NOTE** To select additional AutoFill commands from the Edit menu, click Fill to select additional fill commands such as Up, Down, Left, Right, Series, or Justify.

1. Select the first cell in the range you want to fill.

2. Enter the starting value that you want to repeat.

3. Position the mouse pointer on the lower-right corner of the selected cell. The fill handle (a small black box) changes to the fill handle pointer (a black plus sign).

4. Drag the fill handle pointer over the range where you want to repeat the value.

Fill handle pointer

Create a Complex Series Using AutoFill

1. Select the first cell in the range you want to fill.

2. Enter the starting value for the series, and then click the **Enter** button on the formula bar.

3. Position the mouse pointer on the lower-right corner of the selected cell, and then hold down the Ctrl key on the keyboard. The pointer changes to the fill handle pointer (a black plus sign with a smaller plus sign)

4. Drag the fill handle pointer over the range where you want the value extended. The destination value appears in a small box by the fill handle pointer.

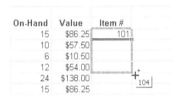

Editing Cell Contents

No matter how much you plan, you can always count on having to make changes to a worksheet. Sometimes it's because you want to correct an error or see how your worksheet results would be affected by different conditions, such as higher sales, producing fewer units, or other variables. You can edit data just as easily as you entered it: using the formula bar or directly editing the active cell.

> **TIP** To edit cell contents using the formula bar, click the cell you want to edit, click on the formula bar, and then edit the cell contents.

> **NOTE** To change editing options, choose Tools ➢ Options, click the Edit tab, change the editing options you want, and then click the OK button.

Edit Cell Contents

1. Double-click the cell you want to edit. The insertion point appears in the cell. (The status bar now displays Edit instead of Ready.)

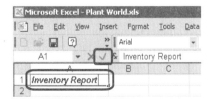

2. If necessary, use the Home, End, and arrow keys on the keyboard to position the insertion point in the cell contents.

3. Use any combination of the Backspace and Delete keys on the keyboard to erase unwanted characters, and then type new characters as needed.

4. Click the **Enter** button 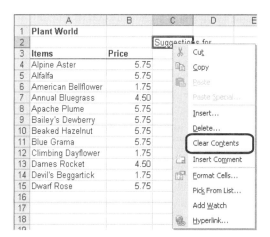 on the formula bar or press the Enter key on the keyboard to accept the edit, or click the **Cancel** button to cancel it.

NOTE You can search for a value or data in a cell and then replace it with different content. Click the cell or cells containing content you want to replace. Choose Edit ➢ Find, and then click the Replace tab for additional options.

Clear the Contents of a Cell

You can clear a cell to remove its contents. Clearing a cell does not remove the cell from the worksheet; it just removes contents from the cell. When clearing a cell, you must specify whether to remove one, two, or all three of these elements from the selected cell or range.

NOTE Deleting a cell removes the cell from the worksheet. When you choose Delete from the Edit menu or from the shortcut menu, you can choose to shift the remaining cells left or up, or to remove the entire row or column.

1. Select the cell or range you want to clear.

2. Right-click the cell or range, and then click **Clear Contents**, or press the Delete key on the keyboard.

Clear Cell Contents, Formatting, and Comments

1. Select the cell or range you want to clear.

2. Choose **Edit** ➢ **Clear** ➢ **All**.

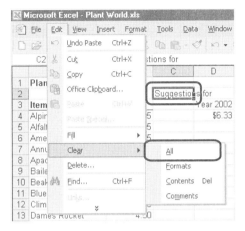

Undo an Action

We all make mistakes. Shortly after completing an action or a task, you may realize you've made a mistake. The Undo feature lets you "take back" one or more previous actions, including the data you entered, the edits you made, or the commands you selected. For example, instead of selecting and deleting the data or a label you just entered in a cell, you could Undo the entry. A few moments later, if you decide the number or name you deleted was correct after all, you could use the Redo feature to restore it to the cell.

NOTE If the Redo button does not appear on the toolbar, click the Toolbar Options drop-down arrow, and then click Redo. Once you use the button, it remains on the toolbar.

♦ Click the **Undo** button on the Standard toolbar to undo the last action you completed.

♦ Click the **Undo** drop-down arrow from the Standard toolbar to see a list of recent actions that can be undone. When you select an action you want to undo, Excel will undo that action and all actions above it.

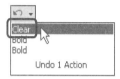

◆ Click an action. Excel reverses the selected action and all actions above it.

Redo an Action

◆ Click the **Redo** button on the Standard toolbar to restore your last undone action.

◆ Click the **Redo** drop-down arrow to see a list of recently undone actions that can be restored. When you select an action you want to repeat, Excel will redo that action and all actions above it.

Storing Cell Contents

Often, you might want to use data that you have already entered on your worksheet. You can cut it or copy it, and then paste it in another location. When you cut or copy data, from non-Office programs, the data in an area of memory called the **Windows Clipboard**. When you paste a range of cells from the Clipboard, you only need to specify the first cell in the new location. After you select the first cell in the new location and then click the Paste button on the toolbar, Excel automatically places all the selected cells in the correct order. Depending on the number of cells you select before you cut or copy, Excel pastes data in one of the following ways:

◆ **One to one**. Excel pastes a single cell in the Clipboard to one cell location.

◆ **One to many**. Excel pastes a single cell in the Clipboard into a selected range of cells.

- ◇ **Many to one**. Excel pastes many cells into a range of cells, but only the first cell is identified. Excel will paste the entire contents of the Clipboard starting with the selected cell. Make sure there are enough cells for the selection; if not, the selection will copy over any previously occupied cells.

- ◇ **Many to many**. Excel pastes many cells into a range of cells. Excel will paste the entire contents of the Clipboard into the selected cells. If the selected range is larger than the selection, the data will be repeated in the extra cells. To turn off the selection marquee and cancel your action, press the Esc key on the keyboard.

With Office XP, you can use the **Office Clipboard** to store multiple pieces of information from several different sources in one storage area that is shared by all Office programs. When you copy multiple items, the Office Clipboard task pane appears, showing all the items within it. You can paste these pieces of information into any Office program, either individually or all at once.

The Windows Clipboard and the Office Clipboard only store the Office program information that you've copied in the current editing session. Both clipboards are emptied when you quit all open Office programs.

Office Clipboard
A temporary area that holds up to 24 pieces of copied information and is available from within any Office program.

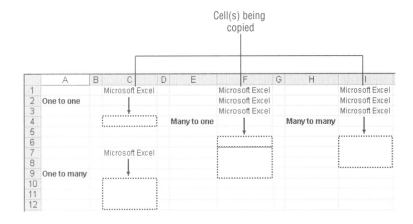

Cell(s) being copied

Copy Data to the Office Clipboard

1. Choose **Edit ➢ Office Clipboard**. The Clipboard task pane opens.

2. Select the data you want to copy.

3. Click the **Copy** button on the Standard toolbar. The data is copied into the first empty position on the Clipboard task pane.

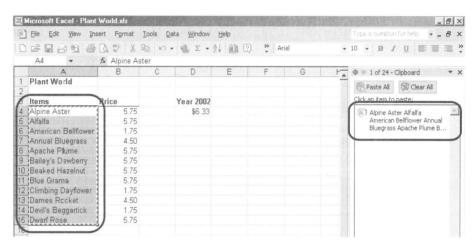

4. Click the **Close** button on the Office Clipboard task pane.

Paste Data from the Office Clipboard

1. Choose **Edit ≻ Office Clipboard**.

2. Click the first cell where you want to paste data.

3. On the Clipboard task pane, click the item you want to paste.

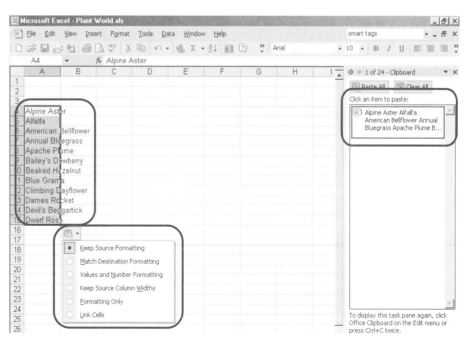

4. Click the **Close** button on the Clipboard task pane.

After you paste an item, the Paste Options button 📋▾ appears next to the item on the worksheet. You can click the Paste Options button to display a list of options on the shortcut menu. This button, known as a smart tag, allows you to immediately adjust how information is pasted or how automatic changes occur. For example, if you have a worksheet with specified column widths, you can paste a cell or range, click the Paste Options button, and then click Keep Source Column Widths to preserve the formatting of the column. Smart tags and their associated choices vary depending on the operation.

> **TIP** To turn on or off Paste Options, choose Tools ➤ Options, click the Edit tab, click the Show Paste Options Buttons check box to select or clear it, and then click the OK button.

Copying Cell Contents

> **TIP** You can cancel a copy or a move while you are in the process of dragging the mouse by pressing the Esc key on the keyboard before you release the mouse button.

Copy Data Using the Standard Toolbar

You can copy and move data on a worksheet from one cell or range of cells to another location on any worksheet in your workbook. When you **copy** data, Excel places a duplicate of the selected cells on the Clipboard. To complete the copy or move, you must **paste** the data stored on the Clipboard in another location. With the Paste Special command, you can control what you want to paste and even perform mathematical operations. To copy or move data without using the Clipboard, you can use a technique called **drag-and-drop**. Drag-and-drop makes it easy to copy or move data short distances on your worksheet.

1. Select the cell or range that contains the data you want to copy.

Copy
A command that creates a duplicate of selected cells.

Paste
A command that places the duplicated cells in another location.

Drag-and-drop
A technique for moving or copying data.

Marquee

An outline surrounding selected cells.

2. Click the **Copy** button 📋 on the Standard toolbar. The data in the cells remains in its original location and an outline of the selected cells, called a **marquee**, shows the size of the selection. If you don't want to paste this selection, press the Esc key on the keyboard to remove the marquee.

3. Click the first cell where you want to paste the data.

4. Click the **Paste** button 📋 on the Standard toolbar. The data remains on the Clipboard, available for further pasting until you replace it with another selection.

	Description	Type	Price	On Hand	Value	Item #
4	Alpine Aster	Perennial	5.75	15	$86.25	101
5	Alfalfa	Perennial	5.75	10	$57.50	102
6	American Bellflower	Annual	1.75	6	$10.50	103
7	Annual Bluegrass	Biennial	4.50	12	$54.00	104
8	Apache Plume	Perennial	5.75	24	$138.00	105
9	Bailey's Dewberry	Perennial	5.75	15	$86.25	106
10	Beaked Hazelnut	Perennial	5.75	10	$57.50	107
11	Blue Grama	Perennial	5.75	5	$28.75	108
12	Climbing Dayflower	Annual	1.75	6	$10.50	109
13	Dames Rocket	Biennial	4.50	2	$9.00	110
14	Devil's Beggartick	Annual	1.75	4	$7.00	111
15	Dwarf Rose	Perennial	5.75	12	$69.00	112
16						
17	Alpine Aster	Perennial	5.75	15	$86.25	101
18						
19						

5. If you don't want to paste this selection anywhere else, press the Esc key on the keyboard to remove the marquee.

> **TIP** Use the Alt key to drag and drop to a different worksheet. Once cells are selected, hold down the Alt key, and then drag the selection to the appropriate sheet tab. Release the Alt key and drag the selection to the desired location on the new worksheet.

> **NOTE** The Windows Clipboard changes when you copy or cut information. The contents of the Windows Clipboard changes each time you copy or cut data. The most recent selection is always the one you've just copied or cut.

Copy Data Using Drag-and-Drop

1. Select the cell or range that contains the data you want to copy.

2. Move the mouse pointer to an edge of the selected cell or range until the pointer changes to an arrowhead.

3. Hold down the mouse button and the Ctrl key on the keyboard.

4. Drag the selection to the new location, and then release the mouse button and the Ctrl key.

	Description	Type	Price	On-Hand	Value	Item #
4	Alpine Aster	Perennial	5.75	15	$86.25	101
5	Alfalfa	Perennial	5.75	10	$57.50	102
6	American Bellflower	Annual	1.75	6	$10.50	103
7	Annual Bluegrass	Biennial	4.50	12	$54.00	104
8	Apache Plume	Perennial	5.75	24	$138.00	105
9	Bailey's Dewberry	Perennial	5.75	15	$86.25	106
10	Beaked Hazelnut	Perennial	5.75	10	$57.50	107
11	Blue Grama	Perennial	5.75	5	$28.75	108
12	Climbing Dayflower	Annual	1.75	6	$10.50	109
13	Dames Rocket	Biennial	4.50	2	$9.00	110
14	Devil's Beggartick	Annual	1.75	4	$7.00	111
15	Dwarf Rose	Perennial	5.75	12	$69.00	112

A17:F17

Copied text appears here

Move Data Using the Clipboard

Unlike copied data, data that you move no longer remains in its original location. Perhaps you typed data in a range of cells near the top of a worksheet, but later realized it should appear near the bottom of the worksheet. Moving data lets you change its location without having to retype it. When you move data, you cut the data from its current location and paste it elsewhere. Cutting removes the selected cell or range content from the worksheet and places it on the Clipboard.

NOTE When Excel displays the Clipboard task pane, you can move the selections that you cut onto the Clipboard, and then paste them later.

1. Select the cell or range that contains the data you want to move.

2. Click the **Cut** button ✂ on the Standard toolbar. The marquee shows the size of the selection. If you don't want to paste this selection, press the Esc on the keyboard to remove the marquee.

3. Click the top-left cell of the range where you want to paste the data.

4. Click the **Paste** button 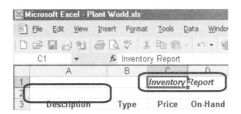 on the Standard toolbar. The marquee disappears. The data is still on the Clipboard; you can continue to paste it until you replace it with another selection.

> **TIP** If the mouse pointer changes to a thick plus sign, reposition the pointer on the edge of the selected range until the pointer changes to an arrowhead, then drag and drop your selection.

Move Data Using Drag-and-Drop

1. Select the cell or range that contains the data you want to move.

2. Move the mouse pointer to an edge of the cell until the pointer changes to an arrowhead.

3. Hold down the mouse button while dragging the selection to its new location, and then release the mouse button.

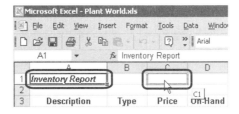

Inserting and Deleting Cells

You can insert new, blank cells anywhere on the worksheet in order to enter new data or insert data that you forgot to enter earlier. Inserting cells moves the remaining cells in the column or row in the direction of your choice, and Excel adjusts any formulas so they refer to the correct cells. You can also delete cells if you find you don't need them; deleting cells shifts the remaining cells to the left or up—just the opposite of inserting cells. When you delete a cell, Excel removes the actual cell from the worksheet, not just the data it contains.

Insert a Cell

1. Select the cell or cells where you want to insert the new cell(s). For example, to insert two blank cells at the position of C10 and C11, select cells C10 and C11.

2. Choose **Insert** ➢ **Cells**. The Insert dialog box opens.

3. Click the option you want.

   ◇ If you want the contents of cells C10 and C11 to move to cells D10 and D11, click the **Shift Cells Right** option button.

   ◇ If you want the contents of cells C10 and C11 to move to cells C12 and C13, click the **Shift Cells Down** option button.

   By using either method, you will replace two blank cells with the data that was in cells C10 and C11.

4. Click the **OK** button.

Delete a Cell

1. Select the cell or range you want to delete.

2. Choose **Edit** ➢ **Delete**. The Delete dialog box opens.

3. Click the option you want.

   ◇ If you want the remaining cells to move left, click the **Shift Cells Left** option button.

   ◇ If you want the remaining cells to move up, click the **Shift Cells Up** option button.

Deleting a cell is different from clearing a cell: deleting removes the cells from the worksheet; clearing removes only the cell contents.

4. Click the **OK** button.

Checking Your Spelling

AutoCorrect

A feature that automatically detects and corrects misspelled words, grammatical errors, and incorrect capitalization, or completes specific terms.

Excel's **AutoCorrect** feature automatically corrects misspelled words as you type them. AutoCorrect includes hundreds of text and symbol entries you can edit or remove.

Add words and phrases to the AutoCorrect dictionary that you misspell, or add often-typed words and save time by just typing their initials. For example, you could use AutoCorrect to automatically change the initials *EPA* to *Environmental Protection Agency*. You can use the AutoCorrect Exceptions dialog box to control how Excel handles the punctuation in abbreviations and word with capital letters, and you can customize the correction of specific words.

Add an AutoCorrect Entry

1. Choose **Tools ➤ AutoCorrect Options**. The AutoCorrect dialog box opens.

2. In the **Replace** box, type a misspelled word or an abbreviation.

3. In the **With** box, type the replacement entry.

4. Click the **Add** button.

5. Repeat steps 2 through 4 for each entry you want to add.

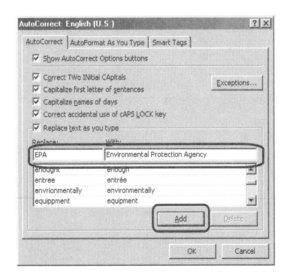

6. Click the **OK** button.

Edit an AutoCorrect Entry

1. Choose **Tools** ➢ **AutoCorrect Options**. The AutoCorrect dialog box opens.

2. Select the AutoCorrect entry you want to change. You can either type the first few letters of the entry to be changed in the **Replace** box, or scroll to the entry, and then click to select it.

3. In the **With** box, type the replacement entry.

4. Click the **Replace** button. If necessary, click the **Yes** button to redefine the entry.

5. Click the **OK** button.

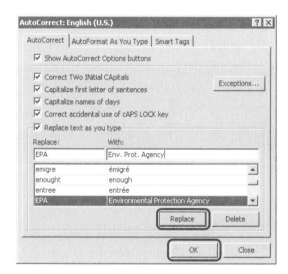

NOTE To turn off the AutoCorrect, choose Tools ➢ AutoCorrect, click the Replace Text As You Type check box to clear it, and then click the OK button.

TIP To delete an AutoCorrect entry, choose Tools ➢ AutoCorrect, select the AutoCorrect entry you want to delete, and then click the Delete button.

Check Spelling

A worksheet's textual inaccuracies can distract the reader, so it's important that your text be error-free. Excel provides a spelling checker so that you can check the spelling in an entire worksheet. You can even avoid future spelling errors on a worksheet by enabling the AutoCorrect feature to automatically correct words as you type.

1. Click the **Spelling** button ![ABC checkmark] on the Standard toolbar. The Spelling dialog box opens when it locates a word it doesn't recognize.

2. If the suggested spelling is unacceptable, or you want to use the original word, click the **Ignore Once** button to pass over this instance of the word, or click the **Ignore All** button to pass over all instances of the word.

3. If the suggested spelling is acceptable, click the **Change** button to change this instance, or click the **Change All** button to change every instance.

4. If you want to add a word to the custom dictionary, click the **Add to Dictionary** button.

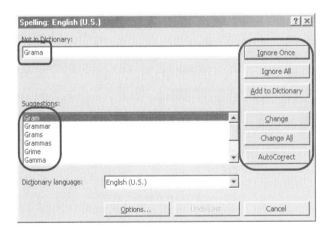

5. When the spelling checker is complete, click the **OK** button.

TIP   To stop the spelling checker at any time, click the Cancel button.

Using Smart Tags

Smart tags help you integrate actions typically performed in other programs directly in Excel. For example, you can insert a financial symbol to get a stock quote, add a person's name and address in a worksheet to the contacts list in Microsoft Outlook, or copy and paste information with added control. Excel analyzes the data you type in a cell and recognizes certain types that it marks with smart tags. The types of actions you can take depend on the type of data in the cell with the smart tag.

Smart tags
A button that helps you control the results of certain actions, such as insert financial information, copy and paste, or automatic text correction.

Get a Stock Quote Using a Smart Tag

1. Click a cell where you want to insert a stock quote.

2. Type a recognized financial symbol in capital letters.

3. Click outside the cell, and then point to the purple triangle in the lower-right corner of the cell to display the Smart Tag button. The purple triangle in the corner of a cell indicates a smart tag is available for the cell contents.

4. Point to the **Smart Tag** button , and then click the down arrow next to the button.

5. Click **Insert Refreshable Stock Price**. The Insert Stock Price dialog opens.

6. Click the **On A New Sheet** option button or the **Starting At Cell** option button, and then click the **OK** button.

Change Smart Tag Options

1. Choose **Tools ➢ AutoCorrect Options**, and then click the **Smart Tags** tab. The AutoCorrect Options dialog box opens.

2. Click the **Label Data With Smart Tags** check box to select it.

3. Click the **Show Smart Tags As** drop-down arrow 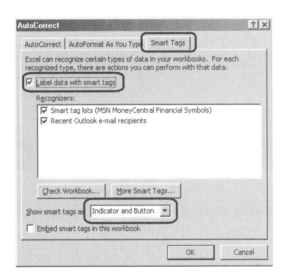, and then click **Button Only** or **Indicator and Button**.

4. To check the worksheet for new smart tags, click the **Check Workbook** button.

5. To save all smart tags, click the **Embed Smart Tags In This Worksheet** check box to select it.

6. Click the **OK** button.

> **TIP** To hide smart tags, choose Tools ➢ AutoCorrect Options, click the Smart Tags tab, and then click None in the Show Smart Tags As list. To discard smart tags, display the Smart Tags tab, click the Label Data With Smart Tags check box to clear it and click the Embed Smart Tags In This Workbook check box to clear it.

> **TIP** Check for new smart tags. You can find additional smart tags on the Web. Choose Tools ➢ AutoCorrect, click the Smart Tags tab, and then click the More Smart Tags button to display a Web page with a listing of smart tags.

3

Working with Formulas and Functions

● ●

Once you enter the data on a worksheet, you'll want to add formulas to calculate it in the way you want. You can create your own formulas or insert built-in formulas, called **functions**, for more complex computations. You don't need extensive accounting skills to build powerful worksheets. Because Excel automatically recalculates formulas, your worksheets remain accurate and up-to-date no matter how often you change the data.

Creating a Simple Formula

Formula
A series of values, cell references, and mathematical operators that results in a calculation.

A **formula** calculates values to return a result. In an Excel worksheet, you create a formula using values (such as *147* or *$10.00*), arithmetic operators (shown in the table below), and cell references (such as *B3:F20*). An Excel formula always begins with the equal sign (=). By default, Excel displays the results of the formula in a cell, but you can change your view of the worksheet to display formulas instead of results. When you enter or edit a formula, cell references and the borders around the cells are color-coded. If there are no squares around a color-coded cell, the cell reference is to a named range.

> **NOTE** When you build a formula that uses cell references, you can click a cell in your spreadsheet to add it to your formula, rather than typing its address. Clicking the precise cell ensures that you reference the correct cell.

Enter a Formula

1. Click the cell where you want to enter a formula.

2. Type = (an equal sign). If you do not begin a formula with an equal sign, Excel will display the information you type as text, instead of using the data in a calculation.

Argument
The cell references or values in a formula that contribute to the result. Each function uses function-specific arguments, which may include numeric values, text values, cell references, ranges of cells, and so on.

3. Enter the first **argument**. An argument can be a number or a cell reference. If it is a cell reference, you can type the reference or click the cell on the worksheet.

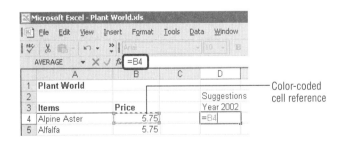

Color-coded cell reference

4. Enter an arithmetic operator (such as * [an asterisk] for multiplication).

5. Enter the next argument.

6. Repeat steps 4 and 5 as needed to complete the formula.

7. Click the **Enter** button 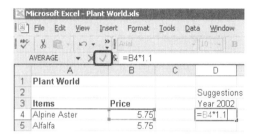 on the formula bar, or press the Enter key on the keyboard. Notice that the result of the formula appears in the cell. If you select the cell, the formula appears on the formula bar.

If a cell contains a formula that breaks an Excel rule, a triangle appears in the top-left corner of the cell. To correct the problem, click the cell with the triangle, click the Trace Error button, and then click the corrective option you want, such as Ignore Error. To error check the worksheet, choose Tools ➢ Error Checking, and then click a button to correct or Ignore the problem.

Editing a Formula

You can edit formulas just as you do other cell contents: use the formula bar or work in the cell. You can select, cut, copy, paste, delete, and format cells that contain formulas, just as you do cells that contain labels or values. Using AutoFill, you can quickly copy formulas to adjacent cells. If you need to copy formulas to different parts of a worksheet, use the Office Clipboard.

Edit a Formula Using the Formula Bar

1. Select the cell that contains the formula you want to edit.

2. Press the F2 key on the keyboard to change to **Edit mode**.

3. Use the arrow keys to position the cursor within the cell contents.

Edit mode
Status bar state indicating that you can edit the contents of a cell.

4. Use any combination of the Backspace and Delete keys to erase characters, and then type new ones as needed.

5. To move a cell or cell reference, drag the color-coded border of the cell or range.

6. Click the **Enter** button ☑ on the formula bar, or press the Enter key on the keyboard.

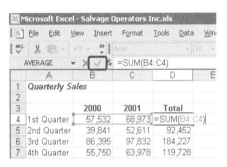

Copy a Formula Using AutoFill

1. Select the cell that contains the formula you want to copy.

2. Position the fill handle pointer on the lower-right corner of the selected cell.

3. Drag the mouse down until you select the adjacent cells where you want to paste the formula, and then release the mouse button.

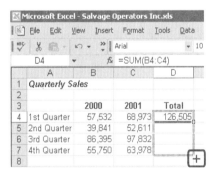

> **NOTE** You can use the Paste Special command to copy formulas only. Select the cells that contain the formulas you want to copy, click where you want to paste the data, choose Edit ➤ Paste Special, click the Formulas option button, and then click the OK button.

Copy a Formula Using the Windows Clipboard

1. Select the cell that contains the formula you want to copy.

2. Click the **Copy** button on the Standard toolbar.

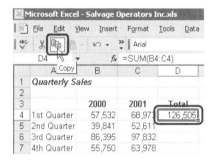

3. Select one or more cells where you want to paste the formula.

4. Click the **Paste** button on the Standard toolbar.

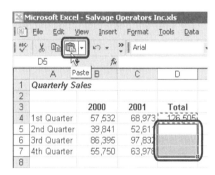

5. If you don't want to paste this selection anywhere else, press the Esc key on the keyboard to remove the marquee.

Understanding Cell Referencing

Relative addressing
The automatic adjustment of cell references that results when a formula is moved or copied.

Excel assumes that when you copy a formula in a worksheet, you want to copy the formula's calculation—not the cells involved in the calculation. By default, the cell addresses in a formula change when you copy or move them to a new location. When you paste or drag a formula to a new location, the cell references in the formula automatically adjust relative to their new locations. The formula is the same, but it uses the new cells in its calculation. For example, when you copy the formula *=D3+D4* in cell D5 to cell E5, the cell references change automatically: the formula becomes *=E3+E4*. This automatic adjustment is called **relative addressing**. Relative addressing eliminates the tedium of creating new formulas for each row or column in a worksheet filled with repetitive information.

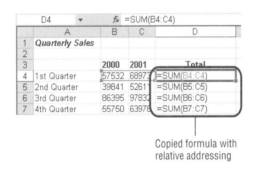

Copied formula with relative addressing

Using Absolute Cell References

Absolute cell reference
An address that locks the cell reference to cells in the formula.

When you want a formula to consistently refer to a particular cell, even if you copy or move the formula elsewhere on the worksheet, you need to use an absolute cell reference. An **absolute cell reference** is a cell address that contains a dollar sign ($) in the row or column coordinate, or both.

Use an Absolute Reference

1. Click a cell where you want to enter a formula.

2. Type = (an equal sign) to begin the formula.

3. Select a cell, and then enter an arithmetic operator (such as + [a plus sign] for addition).

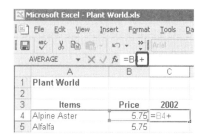

4. Select another cell, and press the F4 key on the keyboard to make that cell reference absolute.

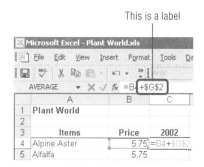

5. If necessary, continue entering the formula.

6. Click the **Enter** button ☑ on the formula bar, or press the Enter key on the keyboard.

Define Label Ranges

It's often convenient to place labels above columns and to the left of rows. You can use the labels on your worksheet instead of cell addresses to reference cells. You can point to cells to add their labels to a formula. However, before you can point to a cell to use its label, you have to define a **label range**. When you define a label range, Excel assigns the row and column labels to the cells.

Label range
A group of row and column labels that you want to use in your formulas.

NOTE
When you adjust the zoom of the worksheet to 39 percent or less, Excel adds a blue border around the labels you have created. The blue border identifies labels at smaller zoom percentages, but does not print.

1. Select the range containing the row labels you want to reference to cells.

2. Choose **Insert** ➢ **Name** ➢ **Label**. The Label Ranges dialog box opens. The selected range appears in the **Add Label Range** box and the **Row Labels** option is selected.

3. Click the **Add** button.

4. Click the **OK** button.

5. Select the range containing the column labels you want to reference to cells and repeat steps 2 through 4.

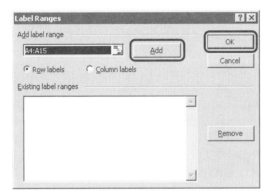

NOTE   If you change the name of a reference label, Excel automatically makes the same change to every formula in which the name is used.

TIP   When you use a label name in a formula or function, Excel treats it as a relative reference. You can copy the formula to other cells, or use AutoFill to copy it and change the reference.

Remove a Label Range

1. Choose **Insert** ➢ **Name** ➢ **Label**. The Label Ranges dialog box opens.

2. Click to select the existing label range you want to remove.

3. Click the **Remove** button.

4. Click the **OK** button.

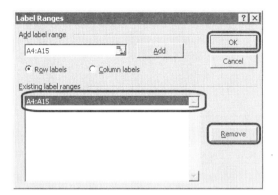

Naming Cells and Ranges

To make working with ranges easier, Excel allows you to name them. The name *Sales*, for example, is easier to remember than the range reference *B4:D10*. Named ranges can be used to navigate large worksheets. Named ranges can also be used in formulas instead of typing or pointing to specific cells. If the cell or range you want to name has labels, you can instruct Excel to automatically name the cell or range for you. If you have already entered a cell or range address in a formula or function, you can apply a name to the address instead of re-creating it.

 Unlike label ranges, which are relative, cell and range names are absolute.

Name a Cell or Range

1. Select the cell or range you want to name.

2. Click the **Name Box** on the formula bar.

3. Type a name for the range. A range name can include uppercase or lowercase letters, numbers, and punctuation, but no spaces. Try to use a simple name that reflects the type of information in the range, such as *Inventory*.

4. Press the Enter key on the keyboard. The range name will appear in the Name box whenever you select the range of cells, but not when you highlight an individual cell in the range.

Select a Named Cell or Range

1. Click the **Name Box** drop-down arrow ▾ on the formula bar.

2. Click the name of the cell or range you want to use. The range name appears in the Name box, and Excel highlights on the worksheet all of the cells included in the range.

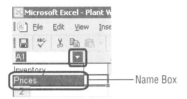

Name Box

NOTE When you select the Ignore Relative/Absolute option, Excel replaces the reference with the name whether the address is absolute or relative. When you deselect this option, Excel replaces only absolute references.

When you select the Use Row And Column Names option, Excel uses the range row and column headings to refer to the range you've selected (assuming a cell does not have its own name, but is part of a named range).

TIP To delete a name range, choose Insert ➢ Name ➢ Define, select the range name, and then click the Delete button.

Use a Range in a Formula

You can simplify formulas by using ranges and range names. For example, if 12 cells on your worksheet contain monthly budget amounts, and you want to multiply each amount by 10 percent, you can insert one range address in a formula instead of inserting 12 different cell addresses. You can also insert a range name. Using a range name in a formula helps to identify what the formula does. For example, the formula =2001 SALES * .10 is more intuitive than =D7:O7*.10.

1. Click a cell where you want to enter a formula, type = (an equal sign) type the function you want to use, and then type ((an open parenthesis). For example, to insert the SUM function, type *=SUM(*.

2. Click the first cell of the range, and then drag the pointer to select the last cell in the range. Excel enters the range address for you.

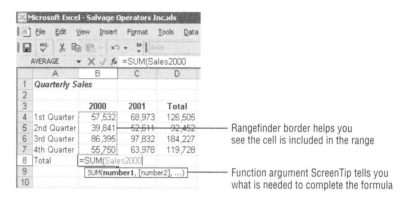

Rangefinder border helps you see the cell is included in the range

Function argument ScreenTip tells you what is needed to complete the formula

3. Add any additional cell references, and then click the **Enter** button ✓ on the formula bar, or press the Enter key on the keyboard. Excel automatically completes the formula by adding a close parenthesis.

Use a Range Name in a Formula

1. Click a cell where you want to enter a formula, type = (an equal sign), type the function you want to use, then type ((an open parenthesis).

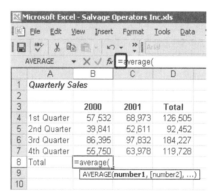

2. Press the F3 key on the keyboard. The Paste Name dialog box opens with a list of named ranges.

3. Click the name of the range you want to insert.

4. Click the **OK** button.

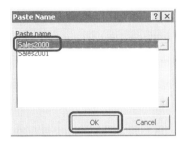

5. Add any additional cell references, and then click the **Enter** button ☑ on the formula bar, or press the Enter key on the keyboard. Excel automatically completes the formula by adding a close parenthesis.

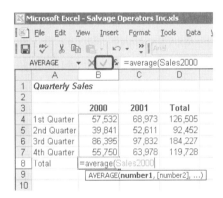

Displaying Calculations

You can verify or check your work without inserting a formula into your worksheet by using the **AutoCalculate** feature. Because AutoCalculate is not a formula that you've inserted, the results do not appear on the worksheet when you print it. AutoCalculate can give you quick answers while you work.

Calculate a Range Automatically

1. Select the range of cells you want to calculate. The sum of the selected cells appears on the status bar next to *SUM=*.

2. If you want to change the type of calculation AutoCalculate performs, right-click anywhere on the status bar to open the AutoCalculate menu.

3. Click the type of calculation you want.

Calculate Totals with AutoSum

You can easily total a range of cells by using the AutoSum button on the Standard toolbar. AutoSum suggests a range to sum, but you can modify this range if you want a different range. You can calculate subtotals for data ranges using the Tools menu and the Subtotals dialog box. You can select where Excel performs the subtotals and the function type.

1. Click the cell where you want to display the calculation.

2. Click the **AutoSum** button Σ ▾ on the Standard toolbar.

3. Click the **Enter** button ☑ on the formula bar, or press the Enter key on the keyboard.

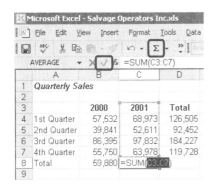

Calculate with Extended AutoSum

1. Click the cell where you want to display the calculation.

2. Click the **AutoSum** drop-down arrow Σ ▾ on the Standard toolbar.

3. Click the function you want to use.

Performing Calculations Using Functions

Functions

Built-in formulas that make it easy to create complex calculations that involve one or more values, performing an operation, and returning one or more values.

Functions are pre-designed formulas that save you the time and trouble of creating commonly used or complex equations. Excel includes hundreds of functions that you can use alone or in combination with other formulas or functions. Functions perform a variety of calculations, from adding, averaging, and counting, to more complicated tasks, such as calculating the monthly payment amount of a loan. You can enter a function manually if you know its name and all the required arguments, or you can easily insert a function using the Paste Function feature.

Enter a Function

1. Click the cell where you want to enter the function.

2. Type = (an equal sign), type the name of the function, and then type ((an open parenthesis). For example, to insert the SUM function, type =*SUM(*.

3. Type the argument or select the cell or range you want to insert in the function.

4. Click the **Enter** button ☑ on the formula bar, or press the Enter key on the keyboard. Excel automatically completes the function by adding a close parenthesis.

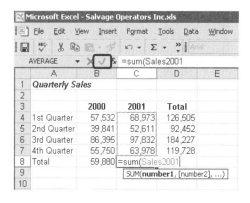

Function	Description	Sample
SUM	Displays the sum of the argument	=SUM(*argument*)
AVERAGE	Displays the average value in the argument	=AVERAGE(*argument*)
COUNT	Calculates the number of values in the argument	=COUNT(*argument*)
MAX	Determines the largest value in the argument	=MAX(*argument*)
MIN	Determines the smallest value in the argument	=MIN(*argument*)
PMT	Determines the payment of a loan	=PMT(*argument*)

Enter a Function Using the Insert Function

Trying to write a formula that calculates various pieces of data, such as calculating payments for an investment over a period of time at a certain rate, can be difficult and time-consuming. The **Insert Function** feature organizes Excel's functions into categories so they are easy to find and to use. A function defines all the necessary components (also called arguments) you need to produce a specific result; all you have to do is supply the values, cell references, and other variables. You can even combine one or more functions if necessary.

1. Click the cell where you want to enter the function.

2. Click the **Insert Function** button f_x on the formula bar. The Insert Function dialog box opens.

3. Click a function you want to use. A description of the selected function appears at the bottom of the Insert Function dialog box.

4. Click the **OK** button.

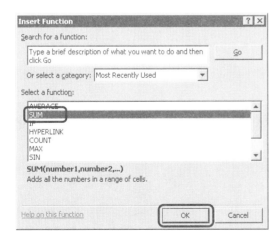

Insert Function

A feature that organizes Excel's functions and makes it easy to create a complex calculation.

5. Enter the cell addresses in the text boxes. Type them or click the **Collapse Dialog** button to the right of the text box, select the cell or range using your mouse, and then click the **Expand Dialog** button. In many cases, the Insert Function might try to "guess" which cells you want to include in the function.

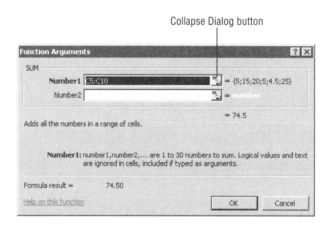

Collapse Dialog button

6. Click the **OK** button.

4 Modifying Worksheets and Workbooks

You can reorganize a workbook by adding, deleting, moving, and renaming worksheets. On any worksheet, you can insert and delete cells, rows, and columns, and adjust column width and row height so that you can structure the worksheet exactly the way you want. It's easy to make changes because Excel automatically updates the worksheet. Whenever you modify a worksheet, Excel keeps current any cell references in existing formulas and recalculates formulas automatically. You can also modify the look of your printouts by adjusting a variety of print settings, including page orientation, margins, headers and footers, and other elements that enhance the readability of your worksheets and workbooks.

Selecting and Naming a Worksheet

Active sheet
The sheet on which you are currently working.

By default, each new workbook you open contains three worksheets, although you can add additional sheets. You can easily switch among the sheets to enter or modify related information, such as budget data for separate months. Whichever sheet you are working on is the **active sheet**. Excel names each sheet consecutively—Sheet1, Sheet2, Sheet3, and so on. When you can rename a sheet to give it a more meaningful name; the size of the sheet tab adjusts to accommodate the name's length, up to 30 characters.

NOTE Although the size of a sheet tab can expand to display a long tab name, a shorter tab name ensures that more sheet tabs to be visible. Being able to see all the sheet tabs is especially important if your workbook contains several worksheets.

Select a Worksheet

1. Move the mouse pointer over the sheet tab of the worksheet you want to make active.

2. Click the sheet tab of the worksheet you want to make active.

Name a Worksheet

1. Double-click the sheet tab of the worksheet you want to name.

2. Type a new name. Excel automatically replaces the current name, which is selected when you begin typing.

3. Press the Enter key on the keyboard.

Color a Worksheet Tab

1. Right-click the sheet tab of the worksheet you want to name.

2. Select **Tab Color** from the pop-up menu. The Format Tab Color dialog box opens.

3. Click a color box.

4. Click the **OK** button.

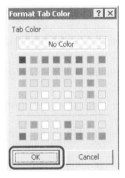

Insert a Worksheet

You can add or delete sheets in a workbook. If, for example, you are working on a project that requires more than three worksheets, you can insert additional sheets in one workbook rather than open multiple workbooks. If, on the other hand, you are using only one or two sheets in a workbook, you can delete the unused sheets to save disk space.

1. Click the sheet tab of the worksheet to the right of where you want to insert the new sheet.

2. Choose **Insert** ➤ **Worksheet**. Excel inserts a new worksheet to the left of the selected worksheet.

Delete a Worksheet

1. Click the sheet tab of the worksheet you want to delete, or click any cell on the sheet.

2. Choose **Edit** ➤ **Delete Sheet**.

3. Click the **Delete** button to confirm the deletion.

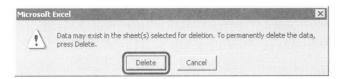

Move a Worksheet Within a Workbook

After adding several sheets to a workbook, you might want to reorganize them. You can arrange sheets in chronological order or in order of their importance. You can easily move or copy a sheet within a workbook or to a different open workbook. Copying a worksheet is easier and often more convenient than reentering similar information on a new sheet.

NOTE To insert a background image in your worksheet, click the sheet tab in which you want to insert a background, and then choose Format ➢ Sheet ➢ Background. Select the picture you want to use as a background, and then click the Insert button. The background image is visible only in that worksheet and will not print.

1. Click the sheet tab of the worksheet you want to move, and then hold down the mouse button.

2. When the mouse pointer changes to a sheet of paper, drag it to the right of the sheet tab where you want to move the worksheet.

3. Release the mouse button.

TIP In order to copy or move a sheet to a different workbook, you must first open the other workbook, and then switch back to the workbook whose sheet you want to copy or move.

Copy a Worksheet

1. Click the sheet tab of the worksheet you want to copy.

2. Choose **Edit** ➤ **Move Or Copy Sheet**. The Move Or Copy dialog box opens.

3. If you want to copy the sheet to another open workbook, click the **To Book** drop-down arrow, and then select the name of that workbook. The sheets of the selected workbook appear in the **Before Sheet** list.

4. Click a sheet name in the **Before Sheet** list. Excel inserts the copy to the left of this sheet.

5. Click the **Create A Copy** check box to select it.

6. Click the **OK** button.

Working with Columns or Rows

You can select one or more columns or rows in a worksheet in order to apply formatting attributes, insert or delete columns or rows, or perform other group actions. The **header buttons** above each column and to the left of each row indicate the letter or number of the column or row. You can select multiple columns or rows even if they are noncontiguous.

Select a Column or Row

1. Click the column or row header button of the column or row you want to select.

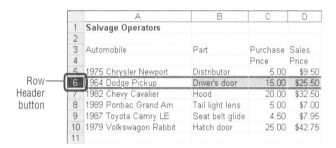

Select Multiple Columns or Rows

1. Drag the mouse over the header buttons of any contiguous columns or rows you want to select.

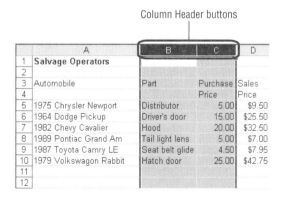

2. To select noncontiguous columns or rows, hold down the Ctrl key on the keyboard while clicking each additional column or row header button.

Select an Entire Worksheet

1. Click the **Select All** button. Excel selects all of the cells in the worksheet, including those cells that do not contain data.

Select All button

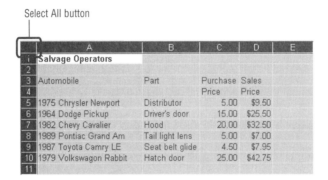

Insert a Column or Row

You can insert blank columns and rows between columns and rows on a worksheet without disturbing any existing data. Excel repositions existing cells to accommodate the new columns and rows and adjusts any existing formulas so that they refer to the correct cells. When you insert one or more columns, Excel inserts them to the left of the selected column. When you add one or more rows, Excel inserts them above the selected row.

After you insert a column, row, or cell, the Insert Options button appears. You can click the Insert Options button to display additional formatting options, such as Format Same As Above, Format Same As Below, or Clear Formatting.

1. To insert a column, click anywhere in the column to the right of the location of the new column you want to insert. To insert a row, click anywhere in the row immediately below the location of the row you want to insert.

TIP   If you are using the AutoFilter feature, you can insert and delete column during the process.

2. Choose **Insert** ➤ **Columns** (or **Rows**).

Excel inserts a new column to the left of the selected column; Excel inserts a new row above the selected row.

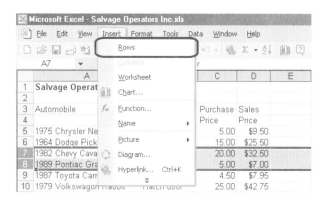

Insert Multiple Columns or Rows

1. To insert multiple columns, drag the column header buttons to the left or right for the number of columns you want to insert. To insert multiple rows, drag the row header buttons to the left or right for the number of rows you want to insert.

2. Choose **Insert** ➤ **Columns** (or **Rows**).

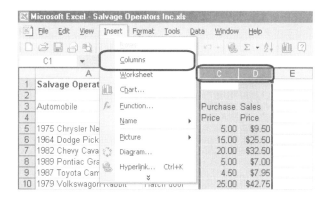

Delete a Column

At some time, you may want to remove an entire column or row from a worksheet, rather than deleting or editing individual cells. You can delete columns and rows just as easily as you insert them. You can choose whether the remaining columns and rows move to the left or move up to join the other remaining cells.

1. Click the column header button of the column(s) you want to delete.

2. Choose **Edit** ➢ **Delete**.

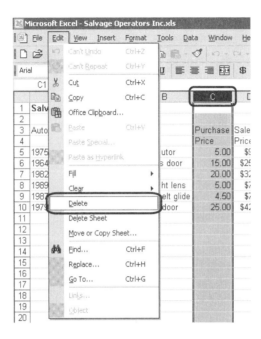

Delete a Row

1. Click the row header button of the row(s) you want to delete.

2. Choose **Edit** ➢ **Delete**.

Hide/Unhide a Column or Row

You may not want all the data on a worksheet to be available to everyone. You can hide sensitive information without deleting it by hiding selected columns or rows. For example, you want to distribute a worksheet that includes employee information, such as address and phone numbers, but the main worksheet also includes their salaries. Rather than copy the worksheet, delete the column, and perhaps need to adjust formulas or formatting, you can simply hide the salary column. Hiding columns and rows does not affect calculations in a worksheet; formulas still reference the data in hidden columns and rows. When you print the worksheet, the hidden columns and rows will not appear. When you save the workbook, the hidden rows or columns will not appear the next time you open it. You can unhide hidden data at any time.

1. Click the column or row header button of the column or row you want to hide. (Drag the mouse to select multiple header buttons to hide more than one column or row.)

2. Choose **Format** ➢ **Column (or Row)** ➢ **Hide**.

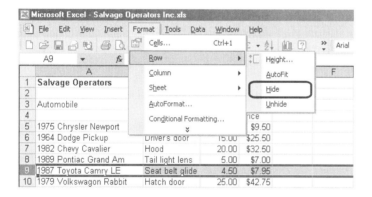

Unhide a Column or Row

1. Drag the mouse to select the column or row header buttons on either side of the hidden column or row.

2. Choose **Format** ➤ **Column (or Row)** ➤ **Unhide**.

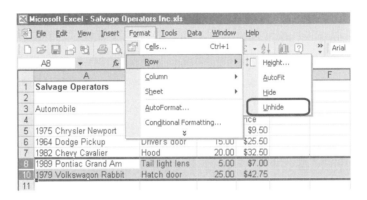

Change Column Width Using AutoFit

AutoFit

A feature that automatically resizes a column or row to the width/height of its largest entry.

As you build your worksheet, you'll want to change the default width of some columns or the default height of some rows to accommodate long strings of data or larger font sizes. Changing the width of a column or the height of a row will enhance the readability of your worksheet. You can manually change column widths or row heights, or you can use the **AutoFit** feature. Excel automatically adjusts column or row size to fit data you have entered.

The Narrow Column ScreenTip shows you the value in a column that is too narrow to display its contents. If a value does not fit in the column, the value displays as ##### in the cell.

1. Position the mouse pointer on the right edge of the header button of the column you want to adjust. The pointer changes to a double-headed arrow.

2. Double-click the mouse button. The column width automatically adjusts to fit the longest cell entry in the column.

Change Row Height Using AutoFit

1. Position the mouse pointer on the bottom edge of the header button of the row you want to adjust. The pointer changes to a double-headed arrow.

2. Double-click the mouse button. The row height automatically adjusts to fit the largest font size.

> **TIP**
> By default, each column in each worksheet is 8.43 points wide, and each row is 12.75 points high. A point is a unit of measurement used to size text and space on a worksheet. One inch equals 72 points.

Adjust Column Width or Row Height Using the Mouse

1. Position the mouse pointer on the right edge of the column header button or the bottom edge of the row header button for the column or row you want to change.

2. When the mouse pointer changes to a double-headed arrow, drag the pointer to a new width or height.

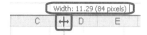

Freeze a Column or Row

Large worksheets can be difficult to work with, especially on low-resolution monitor settings or small monitor screens. When you scroll down to see the bottom of the worksheet, you can no longer see the column labels at the top of the worksheet, which makes it visually confusing to add or edit data. Instead of repeatedly scrolling up and down, you can temporarily fix, or **freeze**, your column or row headings so that you can see them no matter where you scroll in the list. When you freeze a row or column, you are actually splitting the screen into one or more **panes** (window sections) and freezing one of the panes. You can split the screen into four panes and can freeze up to two of these panes. You can edit the data in a frozen pane just as you do any Excel data. The cells in a frozen pane remain stationary when you use the scroll bars; you can scroll only in the unfrozen portion of the screen.

Freeze
A feature that temporarily fixes column or row headings so they are always visible on the screen.

Panes
Individual window sections.

1. Select the column to the right of the columns you want to freeze, or select the row below the rows you want to freeze. To freeze both the column and the row, click the cell to the right and below the column and row you want to freeze.

2. Choose **Window** ➢ **Freeze Panes**.

◆ When you freeze a pane horizontally, all the rows *above* the active cell freeze. When you freeze a pane vertically, all the columns to the *left* of the active cell freeze.

◆ When you freeze a pane, the printed version of your worksheet is not affected.

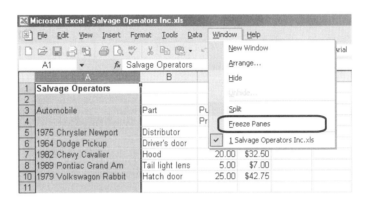

Unfreeze a Column or Row

1. Choose **Window** ➢ **Unfreeze Panes**.

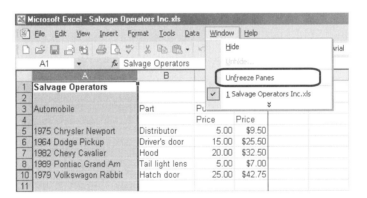

Inserting and Moving Page Breaks

If you want to print a worksheet that is larger than one page, Excel divides it into pages by inserting **automatic page breaks**. Excel breaks pages based on the paper size, margin settings, and scaling options you set. You can change the rows or columns that are printed on the page by inserting **horizontal** or **vertical page breaks**. In **page break preview**, you can view the page breaks and move them by dragging them to a different location on the worksheet.

> **NOTE** To remove a page break, select the column or row next to the page break, choose Insert ➢ Remove Page Break.

Insert a Page Break

1. To insert a vertical page break, click the column header button to the right of the location where you want to insert a page break.

Other page break options include a horizontal page break and a **new page break**.

   ♦ Horizontal page break: click the row header button below the location where you want to insert a page break.

   ♦ New page break: click the cell below and to the right of the location where you want a new page.

2. Choose **Insert ➢ Page Break**.

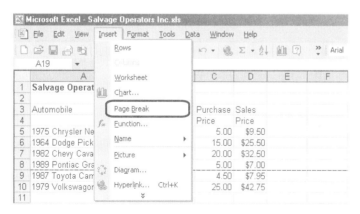

Automatic page breaks
A control that Excel automatically inserts to begin a new page.

Horizontal or vertical page breaks
Controls that let you determine where a new page will begin.

Page break preview
A feature that lets you move page breaks as you view your work.

New page break
A control that inserts a page break below and to the right of the selected cell.

Preview and Move a Page Break

1. Choose **View ➢ Page Break Preview**. The Page Break Preview view opens.

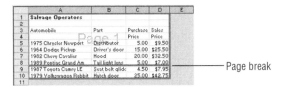

Page break

2. To move a page break to a new location, place the mouse pointer over the page break, and then drag the line to a new location.

3. Choose **View ➢ Normal** to return to normal editing mode.

Setting Up the Page

You can set up the worksheet page to print just the way you want. With the Page Setup dialog box, you can choose the **page orientation**, which determines whether Excel prints the worksheet data vertically or horizontally. You can also adjust the **print scaling** (to reduce or enlarge the size of printed characters), change the **paper size** (to match the size of paper in your printer), and resize or realign the left, right, top, and bottom **margins** (the blank areas along each edge of the paper).

> **NOTE** Changes made in the Page Setup dialog box are not reflected in the worksheet window. You can see them only when you preview or print the worksheet.

1. Choose **File ➢ Page Setup**. The Page Setup dialog box opens.

2. Click the **Page** tab.

3. Click the **Portrait** (8.5 x 11 inches) option button (the default) or click the **Landscape** (11 x 8.5 inches) option button to select page orientation.

Page orientation
Determines how the worksheet data is arranged on the page when you print it—vertically or horizontally.

Print scaling
Resizes text and graphics to fit a specific paper size.

Paper size
The physical dimensions of the paper on which data is printed.

Margins
The blank area at the top, bottom, left, and right of the page.

4. Click the **OK** button.

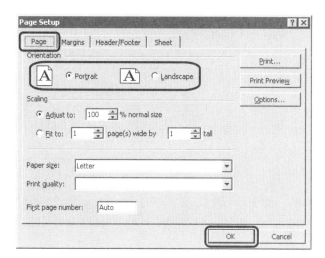

Change the Margin Settings

1. Choose **File** ➢ **Page Setup**. The Page Setup dialog box opens.

2. Click the **Margins** tab.

   ♦ Click the **Top**, **Bottom**, **Left**, and **Right** up or down arrows to adjust the margins.

   ♦ Click the **Center On Page** check boxes to automatically center data relative to the left and right margins (horizontally) or the top and bottom margins (vertically).

3. Click the **OK** button.

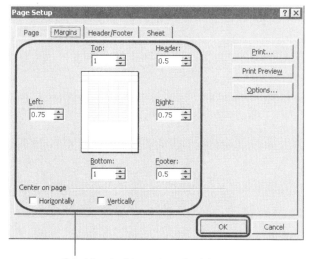

Select the check boxes to center data on page

Change a Header or Footer

Adding a header or footer to a workbook is a convenient way to make your printout easier for readers to follow. Using the Page Setup command, you can add information such as page numbers, the worksheet title, or current date at the top and bottom of each page or section of a worksheet or workbook. Using the Custom Header and Custom Footer buttons, you can include information such as your computer's system date and time, the name of the workbook and sheet, a graphic, and other custom information.

> **NOTE**   To preview the header and footer, click the Print Preview button on the Standard toolbar.

1. Choose **File ➢ Page Setup**. The Page Setup dialog box opens.

2. Click the **Header/Footer** tab.

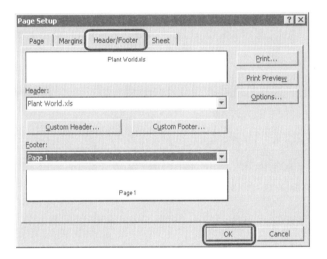

3. If the Header box doesn't contain the information you want, click the **Custom Header**.

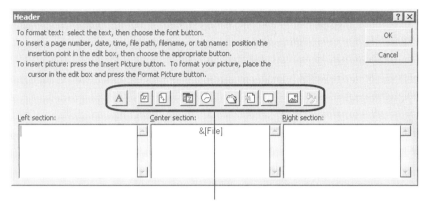

Type custom header text in a section or
press an icon to insert a built-in option

4. Type the information in the left, middle, or right section text boxes, or click a button to insert built-in header information. If you don't want a header to appear at all, delete the text and codes in the text boxes.

5. Select the text you want to format, and then click the **Font** button. The Font dialog box opens. Excel will use the default font, Arial, unless you change it.

6. Click the **OK** button.

6. If the Footer box doesn't contain the information that you want, click the **Custom Footer** button.

7. Type information in the left, middle, or right text boxes, or click a button icon to insert the built-in footer information.

8. Click the **OK** button twice.

TIP To insert a picture in a header or footer, choose View ➢ Header and Footer, click the Customer Header or Custom Footer button, click the Insert Picture button, and then double-click a picture.

Print Part of a Worksheet

Print titles

Column and row titles that Excel prints on each page.

When you're ready to print your worksheet, you can choose several printing options. You can print all or part of any worksheet and control the appearance of many features, such as whether gridlines are displayed, whether column letters and row numbers are displayed, and whether to include **print titles**, which are the columns and rows that repeat on each page.

> **TIP** If you have already set a print area, you do not need to select it. When set a print area, it appears in the Print Area box on the Sheet tab of the Page Setup dialog box.

1. Choose **File** ➢ **Page Setup**. The Page Setup dialog box opens.

2. Click the **Sheet** tab.

3. Click in the **Print Area** box, and then type the range you want to print. You can also click the **Collapse Dialog** button, select the cells you want to print, and then click the **Expand Dialog** button to restore the dialog box.

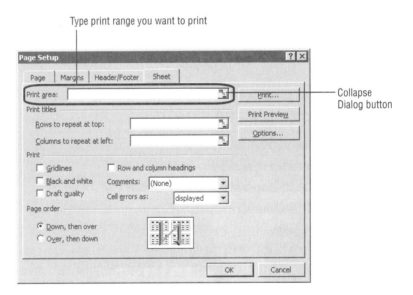

Type print range you want to print

Collapse Dialog button

4. Click the **OK** button.

Print Row and Column Titles on Each Page

1. Choose **File** ➢ **Page Setup**. The Page Setup dialog box opens.

2. Click the **Sheet** tab.

3. Enter the number of the row or the letter of the column that contains the titles. You can also click the appropriate **Collapse Dialog** button, select the row or column with the mouse, and then click the **Expand Dialog** box to restore the dialog box.

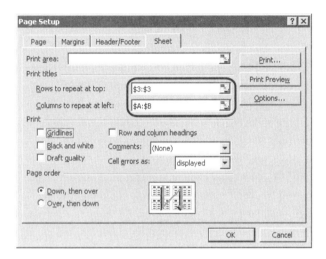

4. Click the **OK** button.

TIP
If you want columns or rows to print on every page, enter them in the Print Titles rows and columns text boxes. Do not include them in the cell range you enter in the Print Area. If you enter them twice, Excel will print them twice on the first page.

NOTE
To adjust the size of printed characters, click the Adjust To up or down arrow to set the percentage size. When you click the Fit To up or down arrow to specify the number of pages on which you want the worksheet to be printed; the size of the printed characters will adjust accordingly.

Set the Print Area

The section of your worksheet that Excel prints is known as the **print area**. You can set the print area when you customize worksheet printing or any time when you are working on a worksheet. For example, you might want to print a different range in a worksheet for different people. In order to use headers and

Print area
The specific range you want to print.

footers, you must first establish, or set, the print area. You can design specific headers and footers for a specific print area. The print area can consist of a single cell or a contiguous or non-contiguous range.

1. Select the range of cells you want to print.

2. Choose File ➢ Print Area ➢ Set Print Area.

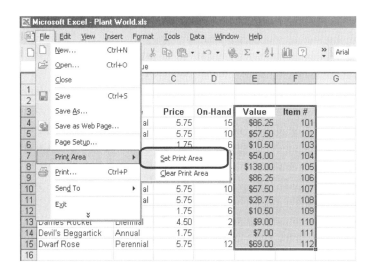

Clear the Print Area

1. Choose File ➢ Print Area ➢ Clear Print Area.

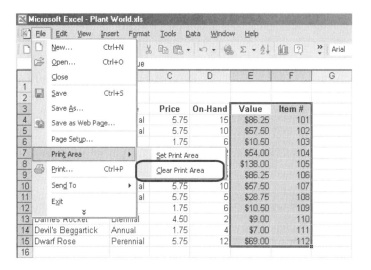

5

Formatting a Worksheet

Excel 2002 offers several tools that make your worksheets look more attractive and professional. Without formatting, a worksheet can look like a sea of meaningless data. To highlight important information, you can change the appearance of selected numbers and text by adding dollar signs, commas, and other numerical formats, or by applying attributes such as boldface and italics. You can change font and font size, adjust the alignment of data in cells, and add colors, patterns, borders, and pictures. By using AutoFormats and styles to apply multiple changes, you can speed up the formatting process and ensure greater consistency among your worksheets.

Formatting Text and Numbers

Format

Changing the appearance of labels and values in a worksheet.

You can change the appearance of the data in the cells of a worksheet without changing the actual value in the cell. You can **format** text and numbers with font **attributes**, such as bolding, italics, or underlining, in order to catch the reader's attention. You can also apply **numeric formats** to numbers to accurately reflect the type of information they represent—dollar amounts, dates, decimals, and so on. For example, you can format a number to display up to 15 decimal places, or none at all.

Attributes

Effects that change the appearance of characters.

Change the Appearance of a Number Quickly

Numeric formats

Displaying values in different formats, such as changing the number of decimal places or whether currency symbols appear.

1. Select a cell or range that contains the number(s) that you want format.

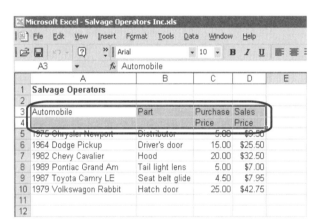

2. Click the **Toolbar Options** drop-down arrow ⬝ to display numeric formatting buttons, if necessary.

3. Click a formatting button to apply the numeric attribute that you want the selected range. You can continue apply attributes as long as you select the range.

NOTE The buttons on the Formatting toolbar are toggle buttons — you click them to turn them on and off. To add or remove a numeric format or a font attribute, select the cell, range, or text, and then click the appropriate button on the Formatting toolbar.

TIP You can format numbers in international currencies. In the Format Cells dialog box, click the Number tab, click Currency in the Category list, click the Symbol drop-down arrow, and then click a currency symbol.

Button	Name	Example
B	Bold	**Excel**
I	Italic	*Excel*
U	Underline	<u>Excel</u>
$	Currency Style	$5,432.10
%	Percent Style	54.32%
,	Comma Style	5,432.10
←.0 .00	Increase Decimal	5,432.10 becomes 5,432.100
.00 →.0	Decrease Decimal	5,432.10 becomes 5,432.1

Format a Number Using the Format Cells Dialog Box

1. Select a cell or range that contains the number(s) format.

2. Choose **Format** ➢ **Cells**. The Format Cells dialog box opens.

3. Click the **Number** tab.

4. Click a category in the list. The options available for each category displays on the right side of the Format Cells dialog box.

5. Select the options that you want apply. You can preview your selections in the Sample box.

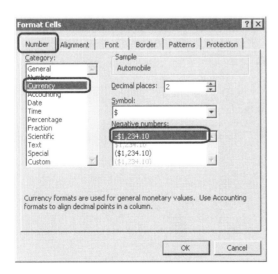

6. Click the **OK** button.

| TIP | To quickly open the Format Cells dialog box, right-click a selected cell or range, and then click Format Cells on the shortcut menu. |

Designing Conditional Formatting

Conditional formatting

Formatting that appears depending on a cell's value or formula.

You can make your worksheets more powerful by setting up conditional formatting. **Conditional formatting** applies predetermined formatting to a cell if the cell meets specific criteria. For example, if this year's sales total is less than last year's, you might want to display the totals in red and italics, but if the total exceeds last year's, you might want to display the totals in green and bold.

Establish a Conditional Format

1. Select a cell or range that you want conditionally format.

2. Choose **Format ➢ Conditional Formatting**. The Conditional Formatting dialog box opens.

3. Select options for Condition 1: Cell Value is, an operator, and the range. If you choose Formula as the format type, you do not select an operator—Excel will determine if the formula is true or false.

4. Click the **Format** button. The Format Cells dialog box opens. Select the attributes that you want apply, and then click the **OK** button.

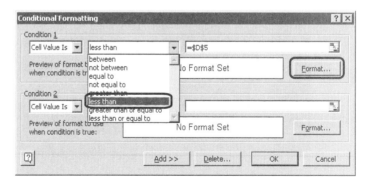

5. Click the **Add** button to include additional conditions, and then repeat steps 3 , 4, and 5.

6. Click the **OK** button.

Delete a Conditional Format

1. Choose **Format ➤ Conditional Formatting**. The Conditional Formatting dialog box opens.

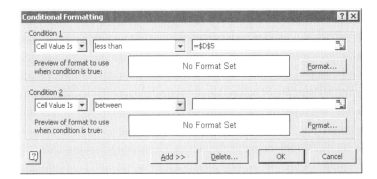

2. Click the **Delete** button. The Delete Conditional Format dialog box opens.

3. Click the check boxes to select the condition(s) that you want delete.

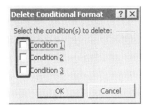

4. Click the **OK** button.

Copying Cell Formats

After formatting a cell on a worksheet, you might want to apply those same formatting changes to other cells on the worksheet. For example, you might want to format each subtotal on your worksheet in italic, bold, 12-point Times New Roman, with a dollar sign, commas, and two decimal places. Rather than selecting each subtotal and applying the individual formatting to each cell, you can **paint** (that is, copy) the formatting from one cell to others.

Paint
The process of applying the attributes of a cell's contents to one or more other cells.

> **TIP** You can cancel a paint command by pressing the Esc key on the keyboard before you apply the paint format to a cell.

Copy a Cell Format

1. Select a cell or range containing the formatting that you want copy.

2. Click the **Format Painter** button 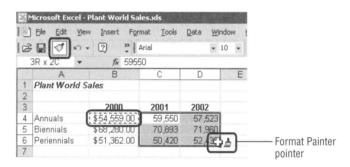 on the Standard toolbar.

3. Drag to select the cell(s) that you want paint. When you release the mouse button, the cells appear with the new formatting.

Format Painter pointer

Changing Fonts

A **font** is a collection of alphanumeric characters that share the same **typeface**, or design, and have similar characteristics. Most fonts are available in a number of styles (such as bold and italic) and sizes. Excel measures the size of each font character in points. A **point** is approximately 1/72 of an inch. You can use any font that is installed on your computer on a worksheet; Excel's default font is 10-point Arial.

> **NOTE** Each computer has different fonts installed. Because users with whom you share files may not have all the fonts you've used in a workbook installed on their computers, it's a good idea to use common fonts.

TIP You can display font names in the Font list as they actually appear. Choose Tools ➤ Customize, click the Options tab, click the List Font Names In Their Font check box to select it, and then click the OK button.

Change Font and Font Size
Using the Formatting Toolbar

1. Select a cell or range whose font and font size that you want change.

2. Click the **Font** drop-down arrow ⬝ on the Formatting toolbar.

3. If necessary, scroll to find the font that you want use, and then click it.

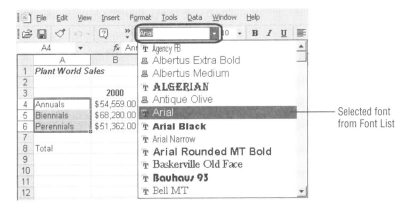

Selected font
from Font List

4. Click the **Font Size** drop-down arrow ⬝ on the Formatting toolbar.

5. If necessary, scroll to find the font size that you want use, and then click it.

Changing Data Alignment

Horizontal alignment
Aligning cell contents relative to the left and right edge of the cell.

Vertical alignment
Aligning cell contents relative to the top and bottom edge of the cell.

Orientation
The appearance of cell text, which can be level or tilted or rotated horizontally up or down.

When you enter data in a cell, Excel aligns labels on the left edge of the cell and aligns values and formulas on the right edge of the cell. **Horizontal alignment** is the way in which Excel aligns the contents of a cell relative to the left or right edge of the cell; **vertical alignment** is the way in which Excel aligns cell contents relative to the top and bottom of the cell. Excel also provides an option for changing the character flow and rotation of text in a cell. You can select the **orientation** of the text in a cell to be vertical or horizontal. You can tilt, or rotate text in horizontal orientation up or down. The default orientation is 0 degrees—the text is level in a cell.

NOTE   You can use the Format Cells dialog box to select other alignment options, but for centering text across columns and simple left, right, and center alignment, it's easier to use the Formatting toolbar buttons.

Change Alignment Using the Formatting Toolbar

1. Select a cell or range containing the data to be realigned.

2. Click the **Align Left** button ≣, **Center** button ≣, **Align Right** button ≣, or **Merge And Center** button ⊞ on the Formatting toolbar.

Button	Name	Description
≣	Align Left	Aligns cell contents on the left edge of the cell
≣	Center	Centers cell contents in the middle of the cell
≣	Align Right	Aligns cell contents of the right edge of the cell
⊞	Merge And Center	Centers cell contents across the columns of a selected range

Controlling Text Flow

The length of a column label might not always fit within the column width you've selected. If the cell to the right is empty, Excel will spill the text over into it, but if that cell contains data, Excel will truncate (cut off) the text. You can format a cell so that text automatically wraps to multiple lines. By wrapping text, you don't have to widen the column, which may affect the appearance of your worksheet. For example, you might want the label *2001 Division 1 Sales* to fit in a column that is only as wide as the word "division." You can also modify cell contents to fit within the available space, or you can combine them with the contents of other cells.

Control the Flow of Text in a Cell

1. Select a cell or range whose text flow you want change.

2. Choose **Format ➤ Cells**. The Format Cells dialog box opens.

3. Click the **Alignment** tab.

4. Click one or more **Text Control** check boxes to select them.

   ◇ **Wrap Text** moves the text to multiple lines within a cell.

   ◇ **Shrink To Fit** reduces character size to fit within a cell.

   ◇ **Merge Cells** combines selected cells into a single cell.

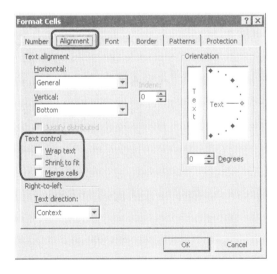

4. Click the **OK** button.

Changing Data Color

You can change the color of the numbers and text on a worksheet. The strategic use of font color can be an effective way of visually uniting similar values. For example, on a sales worksheet you might want to display sales in blue and returns in red.

> **NOTE** The Font Color button on the Formatting toolbar displays the last font color you used. To apply this color to another selection, simply click the button.

Change Font Color Using the Formatting Toolbar

1. Select a cell or range that contains the text you want change.

2. Click the **Font Color** drop-down arrow 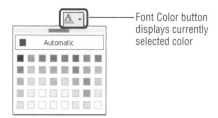 on the Formatting toolbar.

3. Click a color.

Font Color button displays currently selected color

Adding Color and Patterns to Cells

You can fill the background of a cell with a color or a pattern so that the data stands out. Fill colors and patterns can also lend consistency to related information on a worksheet. For example, on a sales worksheet, you can format the second-quarter sales figures with a blue background and the fourth-quarter sales with a yellow background so that each group is easily identifiable. You can use fill colors and patterns in conjunction with text attributes, fonts, and font colors to further enhance the appearance of your worksheet.

When you paint a format using the Format Painter button on the Standard toolbar, Excel also copies the fill colors and patterns to the selected cell or range.

Preview your worksheet before you print it, especially if you don't have a color printer. Some colors and patterns look great on the screen, but can make a worksheet difficult to read when they're printed in black and white or if the color print quality is low.

Choose a Fill Color Using the Formatting Toolbar

1. Select a cell or range.

2. Click the **Fill Color** drop-down arrow 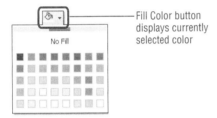 on the Formatting toolbar.

3. Click a color.

Fill Color button displays currently selected color

Adding Borders to Cells

You've probably noticed the light gray grid that displays on the worksheet screen and discovered that it helps your eyes track from cell to cell. By default, Excel does not include this grid on printouts, but you can choose to print grid-lines or alter on the grid pattern by adding different types of borders to a worksheet. You can add borders of varying line widths and colors to some or all sides of a single cell or cell range.

NOTE You can use the Format Cells command to format a border. To apply a border color other than the default (black), select the range to which you want to apply a border. Right-click the range, then choose Format Cells, and then click the Border tab. Select the color you want for the border from the color palette, and then click the OK button.

TIP To place a border around the entire worksheet, click the Select All button at the top left of your worksheet, and then apply the border.

Apply a Border Using the Formatting Toolbar

1. Select a cell or range to which you want to apply a border.

2. Click the **Borders** button drop-down arrow ⬚▾ on the Formatting toolbar to select a border. The most recently selected style displays on the **Borders** button.

3. Select a border from the border palette.

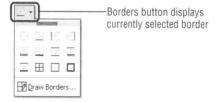
Borders button displays currently selected border

Formatting Data with AutoFormat

AutoFormat
Pre-designed format that you can apply to data ranges, and include numeric formats and font attributes.

Formatting worksheet data can be a lot of fun but also very time-consuming. To make formatting data more efficient, Excel includes 18 AutoFormats. An **AutoFormat** includes a combination of fill colors and patterns, numeric formats, font attributes, borders, and font colors that are professionally designed to enhance your worksheets. If you don't select any cells before choosing the AutoFormat command, Excel will "guess" which data should be formatted.

TIP AutoFormat override previous formatting. When you apply an AutoFormat, it erases any existing formatting.

Apply an AutoFormat

1. Select a cell or range to which you want to apply an AutoFormat, or skip this step if you want Excel to "guess" which cells to format.

2. Choose **Format ➢ AutoFormat**. The AutoFormat dialog box opens and displays samples of each AutoFormat style.

3. Click an AutoFormat in the list. Refer to each sample to see the type of formatting that will apply.

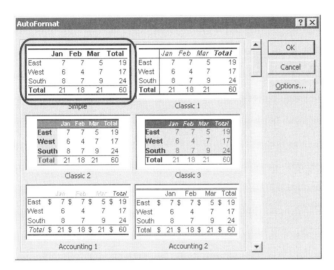

4. Click the **OK** button.

Modifying an AutoFormat

AutoFormats give your worksheet a professional look, but you may need to modify an AutoFormat to better suit the needs of a particular project. For example, the AutoFormat you want to apply might be perfect except that the font doesn't match the font in the rest of your report. You can modify the individual elements that Excel applies to the worksheet. These changes affect the current worksheet only—you can't permanently alter an AutoFormat.

Select AutoFormat Options

1. Select a cell or range whose AutoFormat you want to change, or skip this step if you want Excel to "guess" which cells to format.

2. Choose **Format** ➤ **AutoFormat**. The AutoFormat dialog box opens.

3. Click the AutoFormat that you want to modify.

4. Click the **Options** button. Additional options appear at the bottom of the dialog box.

5. Click one or more **Formats To Apply** check boxes to turn a feature on or off.

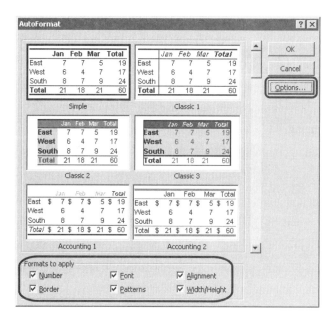

6. Click the **OK** button.

Creating and Applying a Style

Style
Predefined collections of formats, including fonts, font sizes, and attributes, that you can apply to cells and their contents.

A **style** is a defined collection of formats—font, font size, attributes, numeric formats, and so on—that you can store as a set and later apply to other cells. For example, if you always want subtotals to display in blue 14-point Times New Roman, bold, italic, with two decimal places and commas, you can create a style that includes all these formats. You can also copy styles from one workbook to another. Once you create a style, it is available to you in every workbook.

> **NOTE** The check boxes in the Style dialog box correspond to options in tabs in the Format Cells dialog box. You can access the Format Cells dialog box by clicking the Modify button in the Style dialog box. The current setting for an attribute displays to the right of the check box option.

Create a New Style

1. Select a cell or range for which you want to create a style.

2. Choose **Format ➢ Style**. The Style dialog box opens.

3. In the **Style Name** box, type the name of the new style, for example, *Sales Data*.

4. Click the check boxes to turn off any option you do not want to include in the style.

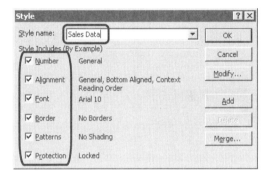

5. Click the **Modify** button. The Format Cells dialog box opens.

6. Click any of the formatting tabs and make additional formatting changes to the style.

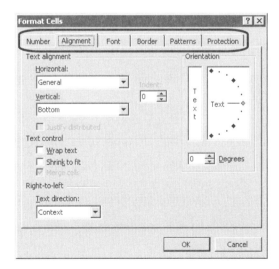

7. Click the **OK** button. The Style dialog box appears.

8. Click the **OK** button.

> **TIP** If you plan to enter repetitive information, such as a list of dollar amounts in a row or column, it's often easier to apply the desired style to the range before you enter the data. That way, you can simply enter each number, and Excel formats it as soon as you press the Enter key on the keyboard.

Apply a Style

1. Select a cell or range to which you want to apply a style.

2. Choose **Format** ➢ **Style**. The Style dialog box opens.

3. Click the **Style Name** drop-down arrow 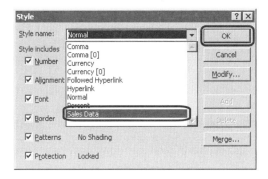, and then select the style you want to apply.

4. Click the **OK** button.

Modifying a Style

You can modify any style—whether it's a style Excel supplied, or one you or someone else created. For example, you created a specific style (fonts and colors) for your division's internal memos. Your company later enacts a style for memos that differs from yours. You could modify your style to include the company's changes. If you want to use the styles created or modified in another workbook, you can merge the styles into the open workbook. If you no longer use a style, you can delete it from the workbook.

Modify a Style

1. Choose **Format ➢ Style**. The Style dialog box opens.

2. Click the **Style Name** drop-down arrow 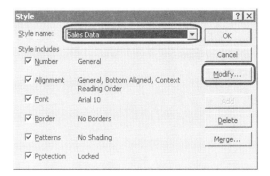, and then select the style that you want to modify.

3. Click the **Modify** button. The Format Cells dialog box opens.

4. Click any of the tabs and make additional formatting changes to the style.

5. Click the **OK** button. The Style dialog box appears.

6. Click the **OK** button.

> **TIP** You can use the Add button in the Style dialog box to use an existing style to create a new style. To keep the original style intact, modify the formatting in the Style dialog box as desired, but then click the Add button and rename the modified style.

> **TIP** To delete a style, choose Format ➢ Style, click the Style Name drop-down arrow, select the style that you want to delete, click the Delete button, and then click the OK button.

Finding and Replacing Formatting

The Find and Replace commands make it easy to locate or replace specific text, numbers, and formatting in a workbook. For example, you might want to replace all the references to cell A6 in your formulas with data contained in cell H2, or you might want to replace bold text with italic text.

Find or Replace Formatting

1. Choose **Edit** ➢ **Find** or **Replace**. The Find and Replace dialog box opens.

2. In the **Find What** box, enter the word or words you want to find.

3. Click the **Options** button to display formatting options. If necessary, click the **Format** button down arrow, and then click **Clear Format From Cell** to clear previous criteria.

NOTE If you want to point to a specific cell format as an example, click the Format button down arrow, click Choose Format From Cell, and then click the OK button.

---

4. Click the **Format** button, specify the formatting you want to locate, and then click the **OK** button.

5. To replace text and formatting, enter the word or words you want to replace in the **Replace With** box, click the **Format** button, specify the formatting you want to replace, and then click the **OK** button.

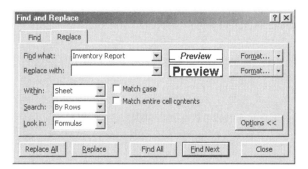

6. Click the **Find Next** button to select the next instance of the formatted text or click the **Replace** button or the **Replace All** button to substitute formatting.

7. Click the **Find Next** button to select the next instance of the formatted text or click the **Replace** button or the **Replace All** button to substitute formatting.

Inserting Graphics and Related Materials

Spice up an otherwise drab worksheet using colorful images that are included with Microsoft Excel 2002, purchased by you or your company, or created by you using a separate graphics program. Graphic images can serve to reinforce a corporate identity or illustrate subject matter in a worksheet. You can add several different types of graphics, such as pictures, stylized text, or an organization chart to your worksheet. From within Excel, you can insert existing graphics, create your own graphic elements, create organization charts, and use WordArt to design stylized text. Once you insert a graphic image, you can modify it to create the look you want by excluding areas you want to hide or by changing its color. You can attach comments to cells—just as you might attach sticky notes to a piece of paper.

Inserting Pictures

Graphic images
Artwork in an electronic file that you can insert from an external source.

You can add pictures to a worksheet, such as your company logo, or you might want to use clip art, which is a package of copyright-free graphics. In Excel, a picture is any **graphic image** that you insert as a single unit. You can insert pictures that you've created in a drawing program or scanned in and saved as a file, or you can insert clip art provided with Microsoft Office or that you've acquired separately. After you insert a graphic object, you can easily delete it if it does not serve your purpose.

TIP To resize a picture so it does not obscure existing data, point to a handle and drag the handle to reduce or enlarge the picture. To move the picture, point to an edge (not to a handle), and then drag the picture to a new location.

Insert Clip Art from the Clip Gallery

1. Select the cell or range where you want to insert a picture.

2. Choose **Insert** ➢ **Picture** ➢ **Clip Art**. The Insert Clip Art task pane opens.

Keyword
Text you enter in response to a search request, which Excel uses to search for files or information.

3. Type one or more **keywords** on which to search, and then click the **Search** button. For example, if your keyword is *plant*, Excel will display images of trees, flowers, shrubs, and so on.

108

4. If necessary, click a collection in the list. The pictures available for the category you selected appear in the Search In list.

5. To quickly insert clip art, click a picture in the task pane. If necessary, scroll to see all the pictures available in the category. Excel inserts the picture in the cell or range you selected.

6. To perform other operations on the clip art, point to a picture, click the down arrow, and then click the command you want to perform.

7. In the Clip Art task pane, click the **Close** button ✕. The Insert Clip Art task pane closes.

TIP   When you select a picture, the Picture toolbar will appear automatically.

NOTE   To add a border to a picture, select the image, click the Line Style button on the Picture toolbar, and then click the line style you want.

Insert a Picture from an Existing File

1. Click the cell or range where you want the picture to appear.

2. Choose **Insert** ➢ **Picture** ➢ **From File**. The Insert Picture dialog box opens.

3. Click the **Look In** drop-down arrow 📷, select the drive and folder where the picture is located, and then click the file you want to insert.

4. If you want, click the **Views** button drop-down arrow ⬛ ▾, and then click **Preview** to view the picture.

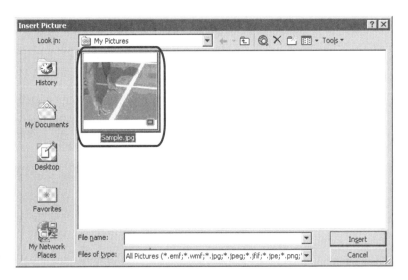

5. Click the **Insert** button. Excel inserts the image into your worksheet.

Inserting Media Clips

Motion clips
An animated picture—also known as an animated GIF— frequently used in Web pages.

You can insert sounds or **motion clips** into a worksheet by using the Clip Gallery. To play a motion clip, you need to view your workbook or worksheet as a Web page. When you insert a sound, a small icon appears that represents the sound file. To play sounds other than your computer's internal sounds, you need a sound card and speakers. You can also insert images from a Twain-compatible scanner or digital camera. To insert an image, you need to connect the scanner or digital camera to your computer and install the Twain device software.

Insert a Clip Gallery Sound or Motion Clip

1. Choose **Insert** ➢ **Picture** ➢ **Clip Art**. The Insert Clip Art task pane opens.

2. Click the **Results Should Be** list arrow, and then make sure **Movies** and/or **Sounds** check boxes are selected.

3. Click the media you want to insert, click the **Insert Clip** button, and then click **Insert**.

4. To play a sound or movie, double-click the selected object.

Click to stop the motion clip

To see how a motion clip will appear in your worksheet, choose File ➢ Web Page Preview.

To display clip art categories, click the All Categories button on the Insert Clip Art task pane. You can also click the Clips Online button to open your Web browser and connect to a clip art Web site where you can download files.

Insert an Image from a Scanner or Camera

1. Set up the image in the scanning device or digital camera.

2. Choose **Insert ➢ Picture ➢ From Scanner Or Camera**.

3. Click the **Device** drop-down arrow ▼, and then select the device you want to use.

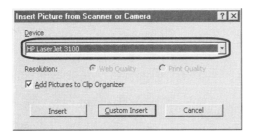

4. Click the **Resolution** option button you want.

◇ Click **Web Quality** if you intend your worksheet to be viewed on screen.

◇ Click **Print Quality** if you intend your worksheet to be printed.

5. Click the insertion method you want.

◇ Click the **Insert** button if you're using a scanner and you want to use predefined settings to scan your picture.

◇ Click the **Custom Insert** button if you're using a scanner and you want to change image settings, or if you're using a camera.

Stylizing Text with WordArt

WordArt

A feature that lets you enhance text by stretching, skewing, and applying special effects to it.

WordArt is a Microsoft program you can use to stylize specific text on your worksheet. WordArt provides a wide variety of text styles pre-designed with dynamic patterns and effects; all you have to do is choose a style and type in the text. For example, if you don't have a logo for your company, you can easily create one using WordArt. You can easily move or resize a WordArt object, even though it might contain many components.

> **TIP** To close the WordArt toolbar or deselect a WordArt object, click anywhere on the worksheet, click the Close button on the WordArt toolbar, or press the Esc key on the keyboard.

Create WordArt

1. Choose **Insert** ➢ **Picture** ➢ **WordArt**. The WordArt Gallery dialog box opens.

2. Click a WordArt style.

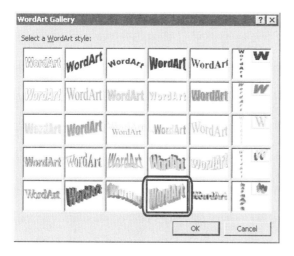

3. Click the **OK** button.

4. Type the text you want in the Edit WordArt Text dialog box.

5. If you want, click the **Font** drop-down arrow ▾, and then select a different font. Click the **Size** drop-down arrow ▾, and then select a different size of lettering.

6. If you want to add font attributes, click the **Bold** button **B**, the **Italic** button *I*, or both.

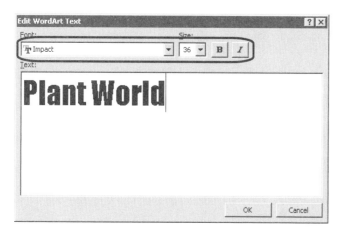

7. Click the **OK** button.

8. If you want, use the WordArt toolbar buttons to make additional modifications, such as spacing, color, and orientation.

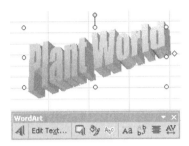

9. To deselect the WordArt object, click anywhere on the worksheet.

Button	Name	Description
	Word Art	Create new WordArt
	Edit Text	Edit the existing text in a WordArt object
	WordArt Gallery	Choose a new style for existing WordArt
	Format WordArt	Change the attributes of existing WordArt
	WordArt Shape	Modify the shape of an existing WordArt object
	WordArt Same Letter Heights	Make uppercase and lower case letters the same height
	WordArt Vertical	Change horizontal letters into a vertical formation
	WordArt Alignment	Modify the alignment of an existing object
	WordArt Character Spacing	Change the spacing between characters

Editing WordArt Text

With WordArt, in addition to applying one of the preformatted styles, you can create your own style. You can shape text into a variety of shapes, curves, styles, and color patterns. When you select a WordArt object to edit the text, the WordArt toolbar opens. This toolbar contains tools for coloring, rotating, and shaping your text. You can also format a WordArt object using the tools that are available in the Format dialog box, including positioning and sizing your WordArt.

Change the Shape of WordArt Text

1. Click the WordArt object.
2. Click the **WordArt Gallery** button on the WordArt toolbar.
3. Click the new shape that you want to apply to the text.

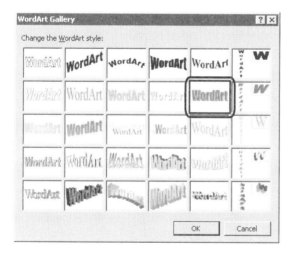

4. Click the **OK** button.

Color WordArt Text

1. Click the WordArt object.
2. Click the **Format WordArt** button on the WordArt toolbar. The Format WordArt dialog box opens.
3. Click the **Colors And Lines** tab, if necessary.

4. Click the **Fill Color** drop-down arrow 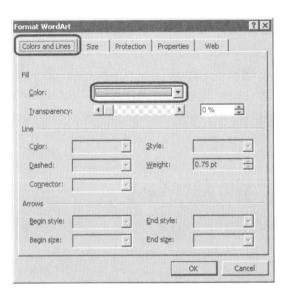, and then select a color or fill effect.

5. Click the **OK** button.

6. To deselect the WordArt object, click anywhere on the worksheet.

Edit or Format WordArt Text

1. Click the WordArt object.

2. Click the **Edit Text** button 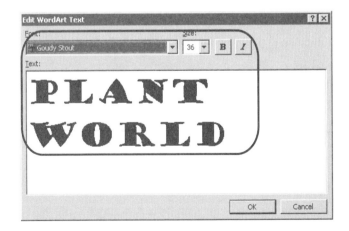 on the WordArt toolbar. The Edit WordArt Text dialog box opens.

3. Click in the text box to position the insertion point, and then edit or format the text.

4. Click the **OK** button.

5. Click a blank area of the worksheet to deselect the WordArt object.

Applying WordArt Text Effects

You can apply a number of text effects to your WordArt objects that change letter height, justification, and spacing. The effect of some of the adjustments will be more pronounced for certain WordArt styles than for others. Some effects will make the text unreadable in certain styles, so apply them carefully. Other effects—such as making upper case and lower-case characters the same height—add an interesting dimension to the text.

Make All Letters the Same Height

1. Click the WordArt object.

2. Click the **WordArt Same Letter Heights** button [Aa] on the WordArt toolbar.

3. Click a blank area of the worksheet to deselect the WordArt object.

Inserting an Organization Chart

An **organization chart**, also known as an *org chart*, shows the personnel structure in an organization. You can include an organization chart on a worksheet using Microsoft Organization Chart. Microsoft Organization Chart provides chart structures; all you have to do is type names in the appropriate places. Each chart box is identified by its position in the chart. Managers, for example, are at the top, while subordinates are below, co-workers to the sides, and so on.

Organization chart
A graphic map that uses boxes to illustrate the hierarchy within an organization.

Create an Organization Chart

1. Choose **Insert** ➢ **Picture** ➢ **Organization Chart**.

2. Click an organization chart box, and then type replacement text.

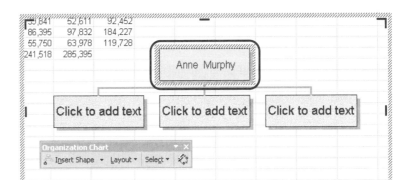

3. To add subordinates or co-workers, click the appropriate toolbar button, and then click the box that contains the individual to whom the subordinate or co-worker reports.

4. To change groups of employees, click the **Layout** button Layout ▾, and then make a selection.

5. Click anywhere outside of the organization chart to return to the worksheet.

> **TIP** To change the default settings for new charts, choose Edit ➢ Options, select the options you want, and then click the OK button.

Use the Style Gallery

1. Click the **Autoformat** button on the Organization Chart toolbar.

2. Click a Style from the Organization Chart Style Gallery dialog box.

3. Click the **Apply** button.

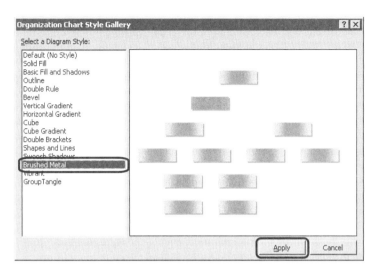

Modifying an Organization Chart

In most companies, personnel and corporate structures change often. You can modify an existing organization chart whenever changes occur at your company in Microsoft Organization Chart. Chart boxes exist in relation to each other. For example, if you want to add a Subordinate chart box, you must select the chart box to which it will be attached. When you add a Subordinate, it is automatically placed below the selected chart box. You can, however, display the chart box levels in a different structure, and you can customize the organization chart's appearance using the formatting options.

Add a Chart Box

1. Click an existing organization chart.

2. Click the **Insert Shape** button on the Organizational Chart toolbar, and then click the chart box type that you want to add (Subordinate, Coworker, or Assistant).

3. Click the chart box to which you want to attach the new chart box.

4. Enter the information for the box you just added.

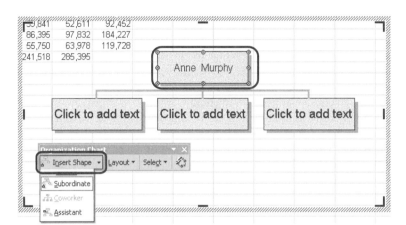

5. Click anywhere outside the box to return to the worksheet.

Change the Organization Chart Layout

1. Select the chart box or chart boxes whose style you want to change.

2. Click the **Layout** button `Layout ▾` on the Organization Chart toolbar, and then click the organization chart style you want.

> **TIP** To change the formatting of a chart box or line, select the chart box or line you want to change, click a formatting button (such as Fill Color, Line Color, Line Style, Shadow Style) on the Drawing toolbar, and then click the style you want.

Creating a Diagram

A **diagram** illustrates conceptual material. Office offers a variety of built-in diagrams from which to choose, including pyramid, cycle, radial, and Venn diagrams as well as organization charts. Using built-in diagrams makes it easy to create and modify charts without having to create them from scratch.

Create a New Diagram

1. Choose **Insert ➢ Diagram**. The Diagram Gallery dialog box opens.

2. Select a diagram.

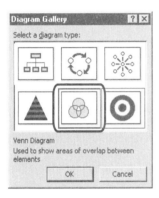

3. Click the **OK** button. The diagram appears in the document.

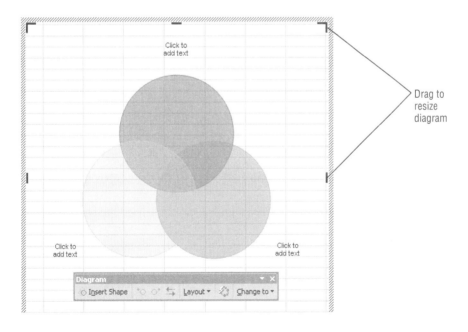

Diagram
A collection of shapes that illustrates conceptual material.

You can also click the Insert Diagram or Organization Chart button on the Drawing toolbar to insert a diagram.

4. Select a diagram element, and use the Diagram toolbar to format the diagram with preset styles, add color and patterns, change line styles, add elements, and move them forward or backward.

5. Click anywhere outside of the diagram to return to the document.

Modifying Graphic Images

Selection handles
Small circles that appear on the edges of an object when it is selected.

Before you can modify or delete an image, you need to select it first. When you select an image, **selection handles** appear on the edges to indicate it is selected.

After you have inserted a picture, you can crop or cut out portions of the image by using the Crop tool on the Picture toolbar.

You can change an image's brightness and contrast. Select the image, and then click the More Brightness or Less Brightness button on the Picture toolbar, or click the More Contrast or Less Contrast button to achieve the desired effect.

Crop an Image

1. Click the image you want to crop. The Picture toolbar opens.

2. Click the **Crop** button ⊞ on the Picture toolbar.

3. Drag the sizing handles until the borders surround the area you want to crop.

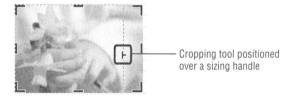

Cropping tool positioned over a sizing handle

| NOTE | Cropping an image does not decrease file size. |

Delete an Image

1. Click the image to display its selection handles.

2. Press the Delete key on the keyboard.

7 Drawing and Modifying Objects

When you need to add pictures to a spread-sheet, Microsoft Excel 2002 is all you need to get the job done. You can choose from a set of pre-designed shapes, or you can use tools that allow you to draw and edit your own shapes and forms. Excel's drawing tools control how you place objects on your worksheet in relation to one another. If you choose to combine objects, you can create sophisti-cated effects.

Drawing Objects

Drawing objects can be classified into three categories: lines, AutoShapes, and freeforms. **Lines** connect two points, **AutoShapes** are preset objects, such as stars, circles, or block arrows, and if you want to construct a new shape, you can draw a **freeform** shape.

Once you have created a drawing object, you can manipulate it in many ways, such as rotating it, coloring it, or changing its style. Excel also provides formatting commands that afford you precise control over your drawing object's appearance.

Drawing Lines and Arrows

The most basic drawing objects you create on your worksheets are lines and arrows. Excel includes several tools for this purpose. The Line tool creates line segments. The Drawing toolbar's Line Style and Dash Style tools determine the type of line used in any drawing object—solid, dashed, or a combination of solid and dashed lines. The Arrow tool lets you create arrows that emphasize key features of your worksheet.

> **TIP** If the Drawing toolbar is not visible, choose View ➢ Toolbars ➢ Drawing.

Draw a Straight Line

1. Click the **Line** button on the Drawing toolbar.

2. Drag the pointer to draw a line on your worksheet.

3. Release the mouse button when the line is the length you want. The endpoints of the line are where you started and finished dragging.

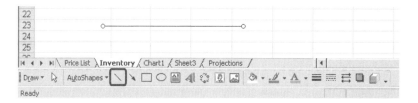

Edit a Line

1. Click the line that you want to edit.

2. Click the **Line Style** button ▤ on the Drawing toolbar, and then select a line thickness.

3. Click the **Dash Style** button ▤ on the Drawing toolbar, and then select a dash style.

4. Click the **Line Color** button ▥▾ on the Drawing toolbar, and then select a line color.

5. Drag the sizing handle at either end to a new location to change the size or angle of the line.

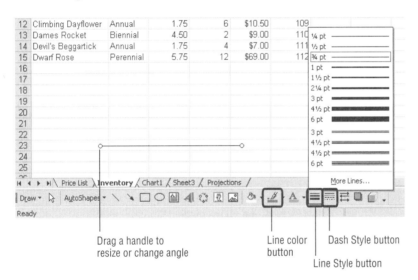

Drag a handle to resize or change angle

Line color button

Dash Style button

Line Style button

TIP You can use keys on the keyboard to adjust lines as you draw them. To constrain the angle of the line to 15-degree increments, hold down the Shift key on the keyboard as you drag the pointer. To draw the line from the center out, instead of from one endpoint to another, hold down the Ctrl key on the keyboard as you drag the pointer.

Draw a Border

1. Click the **Borders** button ▭▾ on the Formatting toolbar.

2. Click the **Draw Borders** button  to display the Borders toolbar.

3. Use the pointer to draw a line on any edge of one or more cells.

4. Click the **Line Color** button 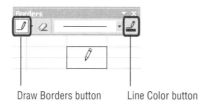 on the Borders toolbar to select a line color.

Draw Borders button   Line Color button

5. Click the **Close** button ⊠ on the Borders toolbar to close the toolbar.

Drawing AutoShapes

You can choose from many different AutoShapes on the Drawing toolbar, ranging from hearts to lightening bolts. The two most common AutoShapes, the oval and the rectangle, are available directly on the Drawing toolbar. The rest of the AutoShapes are organized into categories that you can view and select from the AutoShapes menu. Once you have placed an AutoShape on a worksheet, you can resize it using its sizing handles (small white squares that appear along the edge of an object). Many AutoShapes have an *adjustment handle*, a small yellow diamond located near a sizing handle, which you can drag to alter the shape of the AutoShape.

> **TIP**   To draw a perfect circle or square, click the Oval button or the Rectangle button on the Drawing toolbar, and then hold down the Shift key on the keyboard as you drag the shape.

Draw an Oval or Rectangle

1. Click the **Oval** button 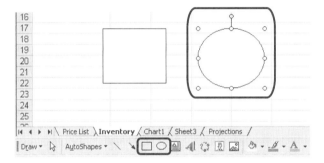 or the **Rectangle** button on the Drawing toolbar.

2. Drag the pointer across the worksheet where you want to place the oval or rectangle.

3. Release the mouse button when the object is the shape you want. The shape assumes the line color and fill color defined by the presentation's color scheme.

Draw an AutoShape

1. Click the **AutoShapes** menu AutoShapes ▾ on the Drawing toolbar, and then point to the AutoShape category you want to use.

2. Click the symbol you want.

3. Drag the pointer across the worksheet until the drawing object is the shape and size that you want.

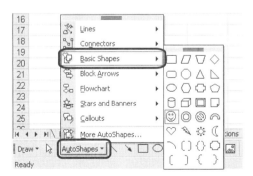

Adjust and Resize an AutoShape

1. Click the AutoShape you want to adjust.

2. Click one of the adjustment handles (white circle), and then drag the handle to alter or resize the form of the AutoShape.

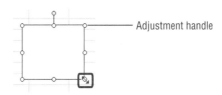

Adjustment handle

Inserting AutoShapes from the Clip Gallery

Clips
Artwork you can insert from the Clip Gallery.

In addition to drawing AutoShapes, you can insert AutoShapes, such as computers and furniture, from the Clip Gallery. These AutoShapes are called **clips**. The Clip Gallery displays a miniature of each clip. You can drag the clip onto your worksheet or click the clip to select other options, such as previewing the clip or searching for similar clips.

Insert an AutoShape from the Clip Gallery

1. Click the **AutoShapes** menu AutoShapes ▾ on the Drawing toolbar, and then click **More AutoShapes**. The Insert Clip Art task pane opens.

2. If necessary, scroll to display more AutoShapes.

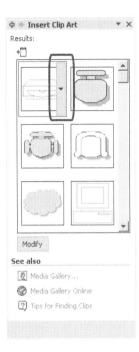

3. Drag the shape you want onto your worksheet.

4. When you're done, click the **Close** button 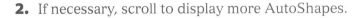.

NOTE   You can import pictures into the Clip Gallery. Click the Insert menu, point to Pictures, click Clip Art, click the Import Clips button on the toolbar, select the picture file you want to insert, select a Clip Import option, and then click the Import button.

Moving and Resizing an Object

After you create a drawing object, you might need to change its size or move it to a different worksheet location. Although you can move and resize objects using the mouse, if you want more precise control over the object's size and position, choose Format ➢ AutoShape to specify the exact location and size of the drawing object.

> **NOTE** You can use the Nudge command to move drawing objects in tiny increments, up, down, left, or right. You can nudge a selected object by holding down the Ctrl key on the keyboard, and then pressing an arrow key.

Move an Object

1. Position the pointer over the object you want to move. The pointer changes to a four-headed arrow.

2. Drag the object to a new location on the worksheet. Make sure you aren't dragging a sizing handle or adjustment handle. If you are working with a freeform object and are in Edit Points mode, drag the interior of the object, not the border, or you will end up resizing or reshaping the object, not moving it.

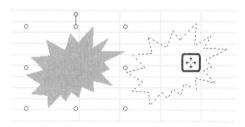

Resize a Drawing Object with the Mouse

1. Click the object you want to resize.

2. Drag one of the sizing handles.

   ❖ To resize the object in the vertical or horizontal direction, drag a sizing handle on the side of the selection box.

   ❖ To resize the object in both the vertical and horizontal directions, drag a sizing handle on the corner of the selection box.

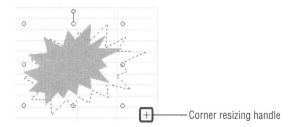

Corner resizing handle

TIP To retain the proportions of the object you're resizing, hold down the Shift key on the keyboard as you drag the object to its new size.

Rotating and Flipping an Object

You can change the orientation of a drawing object by rotating or flipping it. For example, if you want to create a mirror image of your object, you can flip it. To turn an object on its side, you can rotate it 90 degrees. Rotating and flipping tools work with drawing and text objects. You won't usually be able to rotate or flip objects such as charts and pictures.

 TIP To rotate an object 90 degrees to the left, click Rotate Left. To rotate an object 90 degrees to the right, click Rotate Right.

Rotate an Object to Any Angle

1. Click the object you want to rotate.

2. Click the **Draw** menu on the Drawing toolbar.

3. Point to **Rotate Or Flip**, and then click **Free Rotate**.

4. Drag a rotation handle to rotate the object.

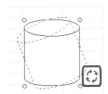

5. Click anywhere on the worksheet to set the rotation.

Rotate or Flip a Drawing Using Preset Increments

1. Click the object you want to rotate.

2. Click the **Draw** menu on the Drawing toolbar.

3. Point to **Rotate Or Flip**, and then click one of the Rotate or Flip commands.

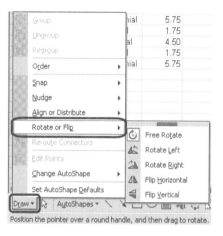

TIP To constrain the rotation to 15-degree increments, hold down the Shift key on the keyboard when you rotate the object.

Choosing Object Colors

When you create a closed drawing object, you can select a fill color and a line color. When you create a drawing object, Excel uses the default color scheme to determine the line style and fill color. You can change the line and fill color settings using the same color tools you use to change a text color. You can also add fill effects, such as gradients, patterns, and clip art pictures.

TIP To set a drawing object's default color and line style, right-click the object, and then click Set Object Defaults on the shortcut menu.

Change a Drawing Object's Fill Color

1. Click the object whose fill color you want to change.

2. Click the **Fill Color** button drop-down arrow 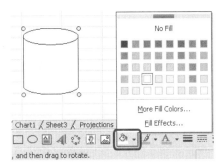 on the Drawing toolbar.

3. Select the fill color or fill effect you want.

Create a Line Pattern

1. Click the object that you want to modify.

2. Choose **Format** ➤ **AutoShape**, or right-click the object, and then click **Format AutoShape**. The Format AutoShape dialog box opens.

3. Click the **Line Color** drop-down arrow ▾, and then select **Patterned Lines**. The Patterned Lines dialog box opens.

4. Click the **Foreground** drop-down arrow ▾, and then select the color you want as a foreground.

5. Click the **Background** drop-down arrow ▾, and then select the color you want as a background.

6. Click the pattern you want from the Pattern grid.

7. Click the **OK** button.

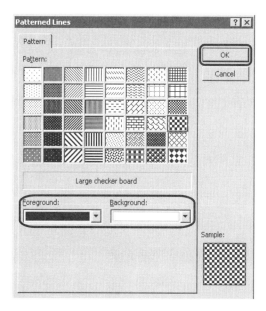

8. Click the **OK** button.

Adding Object Shadows

You can give objects on your worksheet the illusion of depth by adding shadows. Excel provides several preset shadowing options, or you can create your own by specifying the location and color of the shadow.

Use a Preset Shadow

1. Click the object to which you want to add a preset shadow.

2. Click the **Shadow** button 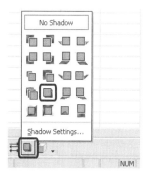 on the Drawing toolbar.

3. Click a preset shadow styles or click Shadow Settings for more options.

Creating a 3-D Object

You can use the 3-D tools to add a three-dimensional appearance to objects. You can transform most AutoShapes into 3-D objects. You can create a 3-D effect using one of the 20 preset 3-D styles, or you can use the 3-D tools to customize your own 3-D style. You can control several elements using the customization tools, including the angle at which the 3-D object is tilted and rotated, the depth of the object, and the direction of light falling on the object.

Apply a Preset 3-D Style

1. Click the object to which you want to apply a preset 3-D style.

2. Click the **3-D** button 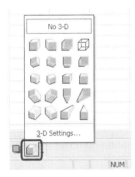 on the Drawing toolbar.

3. Click a preset 3-D styles or click 3-D Settings for more options.

Aligning and Distributing Objects

When you work with two or more similar objects, you need to ensure that they look good on the worksheet. Objects often look best when you align them in relation to each other. For example, you can align three objects so that the tops of all three objects line up along an invisible line. Other times, you may want to distribute objects evenly across an area. Excel includes commands to distribute your items horizontally and vertically, and you can specify whether you want to distribute objects in their currently occupied space or across the entire worksheet.

TIP If the Drawing toolbar is not open, choose View ➤ Toolbars ➤ Drawing.

Align Objects

1. Hold down the Shift key on the keyboard while you click the objects that you want to align.

2. Click the **Draw** menu on the Drawing toolbar, and then point to **Align Or Distribute**.

3. Click the alignment option you want.

   ◇ **Align Left** lines up the left edges of the selected objects.

   ◇ **Align Center** lines up the centers of the selected objects.

   ◇ **Align Right** lines up the right edges of the selected objects.

   ◇ **Align Top** lines up the top edges of the selected objects.

   ◇ **Align Middle** lines up horizontally the middles of the selected objects.

   ◇ **Align Bottom** lines up the bottom edges of the selected objects.

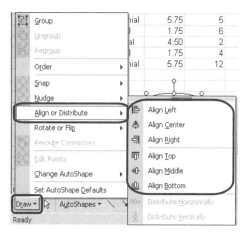

NOTE When you drag an object, you can instruct Excel to snap the object you're dragging to another object or to an invisible grid on the worksheet. Click the Draw menu on the Drawing toolbar, point to Snap, and then click To Grid or To Shape.

Arranging and Grouping Objects

You can insert multiple objects in a worksheet and create interesting effects by adjusting how they interact with each other. If you overlap the objects, Excel will place the most recently created object on top of the others. You can also change the order of the objects in the stack. You can group several objects so that you can move, resize, or copy them as a single unit.

Change the Order of Objects

1. Click the drawing object you want to place.

2. Click the **Draw** menu on the Drawing toolbar, and then point to **Order**.

3. Click the stacking option you want.

❖ Click **Bring To Front** or **Send To Back** to move the drawing to the top or bottom of the stack.

❖ Click **Bring Forward** or **Bring Backward** to move a drawing up or back one location in the stack.

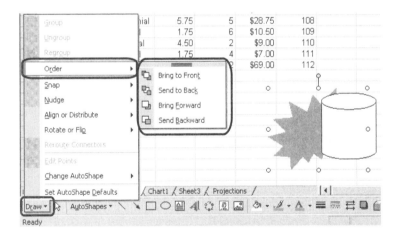

Group Objects Together

1. Hold down the Shift key on the keyboard while you click the objects that you want to group.

2. Click the **Draw** menu on the Drawing toolbar.

3. Click **Group**.

> **TIP** Align objects before you group them in order to ensure the best visual effect.

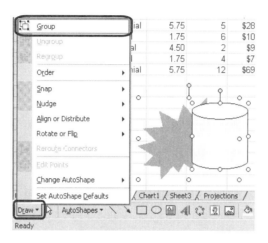

Ungroup a Drawing

1. Select the object you want to ungroup.

2. Click the **Draw** menu on the Drawing toolbar.

3. Click **Ungroup**.

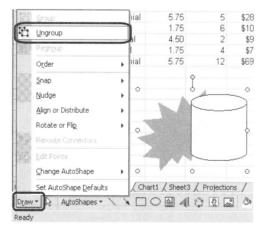

8 Creating Charts

When you're ready to share data with others, a worksheet might not be the most effective way to present the information. A page full of numbers, even if formatted attractively, can be difficult to understand and probably a little boring. Microsoft Excel 2002 makes it easy to create and modify charts so that you can effectively present your information. A chart, also called a graph, is a visual representation of selected data in your worksheet. A well-designed chart draws the reader's attention to important data by illustrating trends and highlighting significant relationships between numbers. Excel generates charts based on data you select; the Chart Wizard makes it easy to select the best chart type, design elements, and formatting enhancements to illustrate any type of information.

Understanding Chart Terminology

Charts consist of many objects. The figure below identifies the elements that you can manage in a chart.

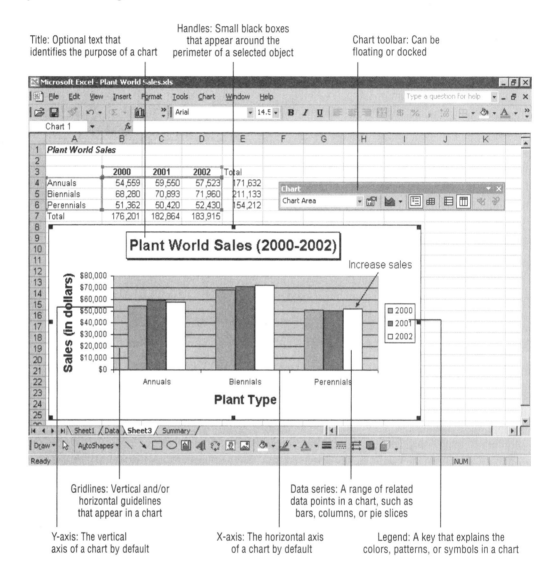

Title: Optional text that identifies the purpose of a chart

Handles: Small black boxes that appear around the perimeter of a selected object

Chart toolbar: Can be floating or docked

Gridlines: Vertical and/or horizontal guidelines that appear in a chart

Data series: A range of related data points in a chart, such as bars, columns, or pie slices

Y-axis: The vertical axis of a chart by default

X-axis: The horizontal axis of a chart by default

Legend: A key that explains the colors, patterns, or symbols in a chart

Choosing the Right Type of Chart

Chart
A visual representation of selected worksheet data.

When you create a **chart** in Excel, you can choose from a variety of chart types. Each type interprets data in a slightly different manner. For example, a pie chart is great for comparing parts of a whole, such as the regional percentages of a sales total, while a column chart is better for showing individual segments, such as showing how different sales regions performed throughout a year. Although there is some overlap, each chart type is best suited for conveying different information.

When you generate a chart, you need to evaluate whether the chart type suits the data you want to plot, and you need to ensure that the formatting choices clarify the information rather than overshadow it. Sometimes a colorful 3-D chart is just what you need to draw attention to an important shift in data, while other times a special visual effect can be distracting.

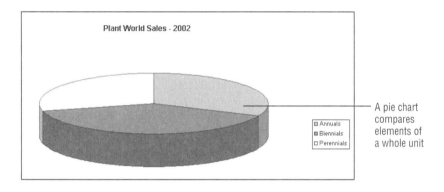

A pie chart compares elements of a whole unit

TIP The Chart Type dialog box briefly describes each chart type.

Creating a Chart

You have to make many decisions when you create a chart, from selecting the chart type, to adding and formatting objects. Excel simplifies the process with a feature called the Chart Wizard. The **Chart Wizard** is a series of dialog boxes that lead you through all the steps necessary to create an effective, eye-catching chart. In Excel 2002, the Chart Wizard includes additional 3-D combination charts and options to format data, multi-level axes, and time-scale labels. After you create your chart, you can always make changes to it.

Chart Wizard
A series of dialog boxes that require your input in order to create a chart.

TIP To move backward or forward in the Chart Wizard, click the Back button or the Forward button. You can click the Finish button at any time.

Create a Chart Using the Chart Wizard

1. Select the data range you want to chart. Include the column and row labels in the data range. Excel will automatically add the labels to the chart.

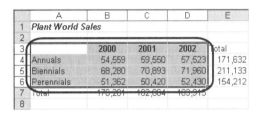

2. Click the **Chart Wizard** button on the Standard toolbar. The Chart Wizard dialog box opens.

3. Click a chart type.

4. Click a chart sub-type.

5. If you want, click the **Press And Hold To View Sample** button to preview your chart as you build it.

6. Click the **Next** button to continue.

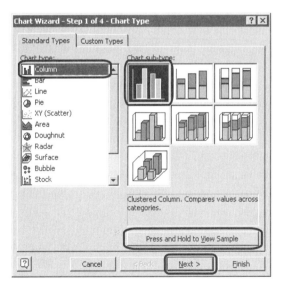

NOTE Before you choose a chart type, try to imagine how your audience will view the chart. Pretend that you're seeing the chart for the first time. Can you easily grasp the pertinent information? If not, how can you improve it?

TIP When you choose to place the chart on an existing sheet, rather than on a new sheet, the chart is called an embedded object. You can then resize or move it just as you would any graphic object.

7. Make sure you've selected the correct data range.

8. Select the appropriate option button to plot the data series in rows or in columns.

9. Click the **Next** button to continue.

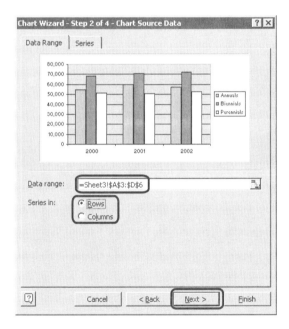

10. Type titles in the appropriate text boxes to identify each category of data. If you want, click other tabs to change additional chart options.

11. Click the **Next** button to continue.

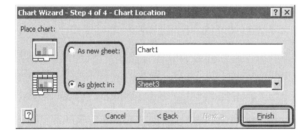

Click tabs
to change
chart options

12. Click an option to choose whether to place the chart on a new work-sheet or embed it on an existing worksheet.

13. Click the **Finish** button.

Editing a Chart

When you edit a chart, you alter its features, which can include selecting data or formatting elements. For example, you might want to use different colors or patterns in a data series. To change the type of chart or any element in it, you must first select the chart or element. When you select a chart, handles display around the window's perimeter, and the Chart toolbar displays on screen (docked or floating). When you select a chart, all of the buttons on this toolbar become active. You can use the ScreenTip feature to display the data value and the name of any object or area on a chart. When you select an object in a chart, the name of the object appears in the Chart Objects list box on the Chart toolbar, which indicates that you can now edit the object.

Editing a chart does not affect the data used to create it. You don't need to worry about updating a chart if you change data in the worksheet, because Excel automatically updates the chart. You can change the data range at any time. If you want to plot more or less data in a range, you can select the data series on the worksheet, and then drag the range to the chart.

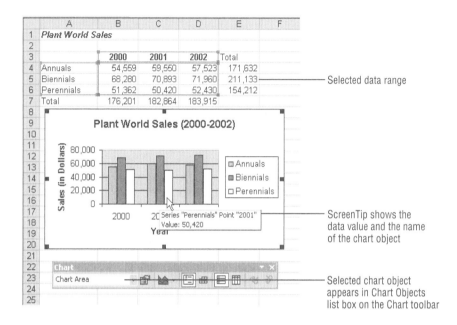

Selected data range

ScreenTip shows the data value and the name of the chart object

Selected chart object appears in Chart Objects list box on the Chart toolbar

Selecting a Chart

You need to select a chart object before you can move it, resize it, or change its formatting. When you select an object, it is surrounded by small black squares, called **handles**. You can also select an object by clicking the Chart Objects drop-down arrow on the Chart toolbar, and then clicking the chart object you want to select.

Select and Deselect a Chart Object

1. Select a chart. The Chart toolbar appears when you select a chart.

Handles
Small black squares that surround the chart when it is selected.

2. Position the mouse pointer over a chart object, click the object to select it, or click the **Chart Objects** drop-down arrow ⬛ on the Chart toolbar, and then click the name of the object you want to select.

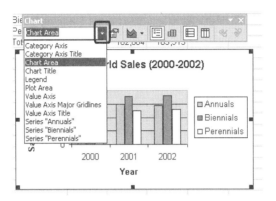

3. Click another area of the chart, or press the Esc key on the keyboard to deselect a chart object.

Changing a Chart Type

Excel's default chart type is the column chart, although there are many other types from which to choose. A column chart might adequately display your data, but you should experiment with a variety of chart types to find the one that shows your data in the most effective way.

> **TIP** To quickly apply another chart type, click the chart to select it, click the Chart Wizard button on the Standard toolbar, and then choose a different chart type. You can also right-click the chart, and then click Chart Type.

Change a Chart Type Quickly

1. Select a chart whose chart type you want to change.

2. Click the **Chart Type** button drop-down arrow 🏔️ on the Chart toolbar.

3. Select a chart type. Excel automatically changes the chart type when you release the mouse button.

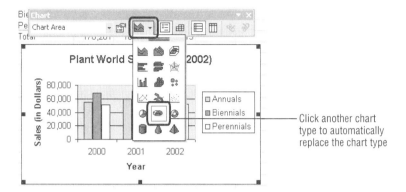

Click another chart type to automatically replace the chart type

Moving and Resizing a Chart

You can move or resize an embedded chart after you select it. If you've created a chart as a new sheet instead of as an embedded object on an existing worksheet, the chart's size and location are fixed by the sheet's margins. You can change the margins to resize or reposition the chart.

NOTE If you drag a chart's handle, you will resize, not move, the chart. If you accidentally resize a chart, hold down the Ctrl+Z keys on the keyboard to undo the change.

Move an Embedded Chart

1. Select a chart you want to move.

2. Position the mouse pointer over a blank area of the chart, and then drag the pointer to move the outline of the chart to a new location.

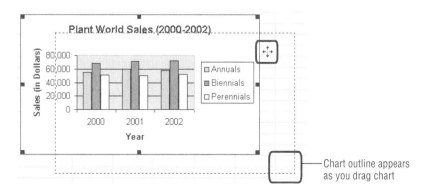

Chart outline appears as you drag chart

3. Release the mouse button.

Resize an Embedded Chart

1. Select a chart you want to resize.

2. Position the mouse pointer over one of the handles.

3. Drag the handle to the new chart size.

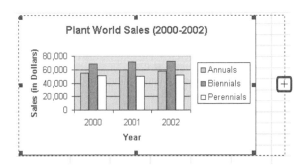

4. Release the mouse button.

Pulling Out a Pie Slice

A pie chart is an effective and easily understood chart type for comparing segments of a whole, such as expenditures by category. You can call attention to individual pie slices that are particularly significant by moving them away from the other pieces, or exploding the pie.

> **TIP** Because a pie chart has only one data series, when you click a single slice, you select the entire data series. To select a specific slice, click a slice a second time.

Explode a Single Pie Slice

1. Select a pie chart.

2. Click to select the pie slice that you want to explode.

3. Drag the slice away from the pie.

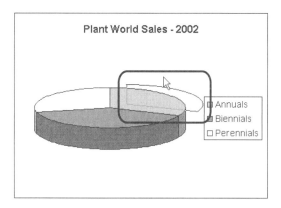

4. Release the mouse button.

You can undo an exploded pie slice by selecting the exploded slice, and then dragging it back towards the center of the pie.

Adding and Deleting a Data Series

Many components make up a chart. Each range of data that comprises a bar, column, or pie slice is called a **data series**; each value in a data series is called a **data point**. The data series is defined when you select a range on a worksheet and then open the Chart Wizard. However, what if you want to add a data series once a chart is complete? You can add a data series by using the mouse, the Chart menu, or the Chart Wizard. As you create and modify additional charts using the same data, you might find it helpful to delete or change the order of one or more data series. You can delete a data series without re-creating the chart.

Data Series
A collection of associated data that Excel uses to plot any chart type.

Data Point
A single value in a data series.

Add a Data Series to a Chart Quickly

1. Select the range that contains the data series that you want to add to your chart.

2. Drag the range into the existing chart.

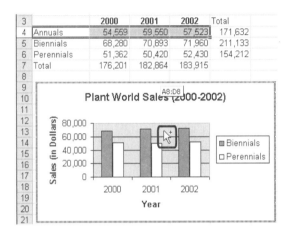

3. Release the mouse button.

NOTE To delete a single data point, but keep the rest of the series in the chart, click the data point twice so that it is the only point selected, and then press the Delete key on the keyboard. Click the Undo button on the Standard toolbar to restore the deleted data series or data point in the chart.

TIP When you position the mouse pointer over any area or object within the chart, a ScreenTip displays the value of the data point, as well as the name of the area or object.

Delete a Data Series

1. Select the chart that contains the data series that you want to delete.

2. Click any data point in the data series.

3. Press the Delete key on the keyboard.

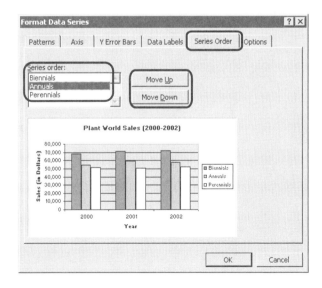

Change Data Series Order

1. Select the chart that contains the data series that you want to change.

2. Double-click any data point in the data series. The Format Data Series dialog box opens.

3. Click the **Series Order** tab.

4. Click the series that you want to change.

5. Click **Move Up** button or the **Move Down** button.

6. Click the **OK** button.

Enhancing a Data Series

When you initially use the Chart Wizard, Excel automatically selects the colors that it will use to represent each data series. You can change one or all of the default colors. You may want more dynamic colors—adding patterns and texture to further enhance a data series. Or, perhaps you'll be printing your charts in black and white and you want to ensure the readability of each data series. You can also insert a picture in a chart so that its image occupies a bar or column.

TIP To format a chart object quickly, double-click an object to open a corresponding Format dialog box, which you can use to change the object's attributes. Depending on which objects are selected, your formatting options will vary.

Change a Data Series Color or Pattern

1. Click any data point in a data series to select it.

2. Double-click a data point in the selected data series. The Format Data Series dialog box opens.

3. Click the **Patterns** tab.

4. Click a color in the Area palette. The selected color displays in the Sample box.

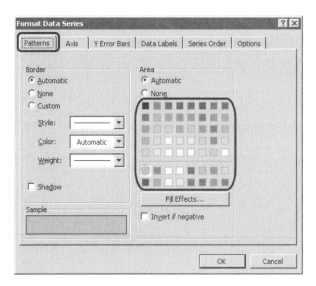

5. If you want to add effects, such as textures, patterns, gradients, or pictures, click the **Fill Effects** button.

6. Click the **Gradient**, **Texture**, or **Pattern** tab to change the qualities of the data series color.

7. When you're done, click the **OK** button.

8. Click the **OK** button if you're satisfied with the results shown in the Sample box, or select different options.

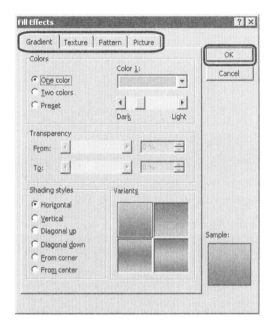

Enhancing a Chart

Add **chart options** to enhance the appearance of the chart and increase its overall effectiveness. Chart options include **chart objects** such as titles, legends, text annotations, and gridlines. A **chart title** identifies the primary purpose of the chart; adding a title for each axis also clarifies the data that you're plotting. Titles can be any length and you can format them just like other worksheet text. A **legend** helps the reader connect the colors and patterns in a chart with the data they represent. **Gridlines** are horizontal and vertical lines that help the reader determine data point values in a chart. You can modify legends and gridlines at any time.

Add a Title

1. Select a chart to which you want to add one or more titles.

2. Choose **Chart ➢ Chart Options**. The Chart Options dialog box opens.

Chart Options
Augmentations and enhancements that you can add to a chart.

Chart Objects
Individual items within a chart (such as a title or legend) that you can select and modify.

Chart Title
Text you can insert to clarify the purpose of the chart.

Legend
An identifier that matches colors or patterns in the chart with data.

Gridlines
Horizontal or vertical lines of a specified width and interval that aid in a chart's readability.

3. Click the **Titles** tab.

4. Type the text you want for the title of the chart.

5. To add a title for the x-axis, press the Tab key on the keyboard, and then type the text.

6. To add a title for the y-axis, press the Tab key on the keyboard, and then type the text.

7. If you want a second line for the x-axis or y-axis, press the Tab key on the keyboard to move to the Second Category or Second Value box, and then type the title text (if available).

8. Preview the title(s) you are adding.

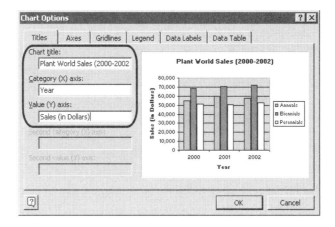

9. Click the **OK** button.

Add or Delete a Legend

1. Select the chart to which you want to add or delete a legend.

2. Click the **Legend** button on the Chart toolbar. You can drag the legend to move it to a new location.

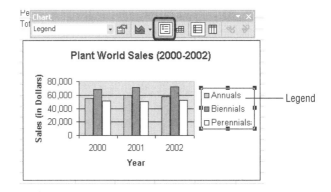

TIP Legend text is derived from the data series plotted within a chart. You can rename an item within a legend by changing the text in the data series.

NOTE Major gridlines occur at each value on an axis; minor gridlines occur between values on an axis. Use gridlines sparingly and only when adding them improves the readability of a chart.

Drawing on a Chart

Once you have added titles and text to your chart, you might want to accentuate the data using tools on the Drawing toolbar. For example, you can apply a drop shadow to add dimension to a chart's title, or draw an arrow to show a connection between annotated text and specific data in your chart.

Add a Drop Shadow to a Chart Title

1. Select the chart.

2. Double-click the title. The Format Chart Title dialog box opens.

3. Click the **Patterns** tab, if necessary.

4. Click the **Shadow** check box to select it.

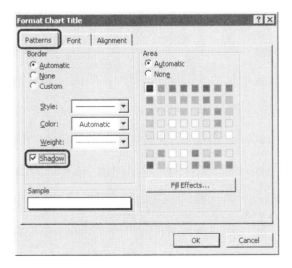

5. Click the **OK** button.

TIP Hold down the Shift key on the keyboard while you drag the pointer to create a vertical, horizontal, or diagonal arrow.

Draw an Arrow on a Chart

1. Select the chart.

2. If necessary, click the **Drawing** button 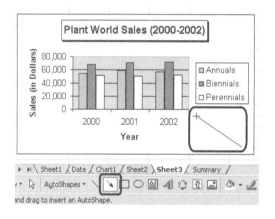 on the Standard toolbar to display the Drawing toolbar.

3. Click the **Arrow** button on the Drawing toolbar.

4. Modify the arrow object. Click the **Line Style** button , **Dash Style** button , or **Arrow Style** button on the Drawing toolbar to modify the arrow object.

5. Position the mouse pointer near the object that you want as the starting point, or base, of the arrow.

6. Drag the pointer from the base object to a target object.

7. Release the mouse button. The arrowhead appears at the end of the line and points to the target object.

Formatting Chart Elements

Chart Text
Objects containing text, such as data labels and titles.

Objects such as annotated text, data labels, and titles contain **chart text**. To make chart text more readable, you can change the text font, style, and size.

You can also change the format of a **chart axis**. For example, if the axis labels or the scale setting is too long and unreadable, you might want to reduce the font size or change the scale to make the labels fit better in a small space.

TIP To change the alignment of the text object, double-click the text you want to change, click the Alignment tab, change the orientation, and then click the OK button.

NOTE You can change the pattern of a chart axis. Double-click the axis you want to change, click the Patterns tab, change the line style, major or minor tick mark type, and labels, and then click the OK button.

Format Chart Text

1. Select the text object that you want to change.

2. Double-click the object that contains the text. The Format Chart Title dialog box opens.

3. Click the **Font** tab.

4. Select a font, font style, and size you want.

5. Select any combination of the Underline, Color, Background, and Effects options.

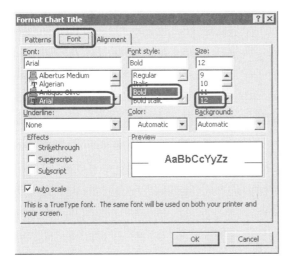

6. Click the **OK** button.

Format a Chart Axis

1. Select the axis that you want to change.

2. Double-click the axis you want to format. The Format Axis dialog box opens.

3. Click the **Scale** tab.

4. Select the scale and display units you want.

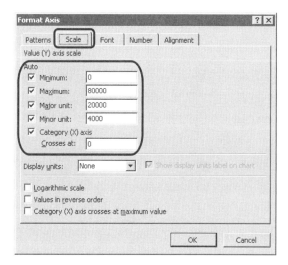

5. To change the number format, click the **Number** tab, and then select the number format you want.

6. Click the **OK** button.

Analyzing Worksheet Data

In addition to using a worksheet to calculate values, you can also use it to manage and analyze a list of information, also called a **database**. For example, you can create an inventory list, a school grade book, or a customer database. Excel provides a variety of easy-to-use tools so that you can keep lists current and analyze your data. For example, you can find out which inventory items are out of stock or single out your best customers. You may want to use data analysis tools that organize data alphanumerically, or that display information that meets specific criteria. You can analyze data directly in a worksheet, or you can use a feature called a Data Form, which is an on-screen data entry tool that resembles paper form. A Data Form lets you easily enter data by filling in blank text boxes. You can first determine your overall sales in a given time frame, and then identify the departments and the top sales people.

Understanding List Terminology

List
A collection of related records in an Excel worksheet.

A database is a collection of related records. Examples of databases are an address book, a customer list, product inventory, and a telephone directory. In Excel, a database is referred to as a **list**, and consists of the following components.

List range The block of cells that contains the list or part of the list you want to analyze. A list range can occupy no more than one worksheet.

Record. One set of related fields, such as all the fields pertaining to one customer or one product. On a worksheet, each row represents one record.

Field name. The title given to a field. In an Excel list, the first row contains the names of each field. The maximum length for a field name is 255 characters, including upper case and lower case letters and spaces.

Field. One piece of information, such as a customer's last name or an item's code number. On a worksheet, each column represents a field.

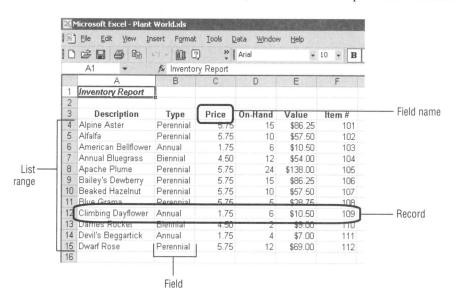

Creating a List

To create a list in Excel, you enter data in worksheet cells, just as you do when you create any worksheet. You can enter records in any order and sort them at any time. When you create a list, you need to follow a few rules:

- ❖ Enter field names as the top row in adjacent columns in a list.

- ❖ Enter each record in a single row, with each field in the column corresponding to the correct field name.

- ❖ Do not include any blank rows within the list range.

- ❖ Do not use more than one worksheet for a single list range.

Enter Data in a List

1. Open a blank worksheet, or use a worksheet that has a sufficient number of empty columns and rows for the list.

2. Enter a name for each field across the first row.

3. Enter the field information for each record in the row, directly beneath the field names. Adjust column width as necessary.

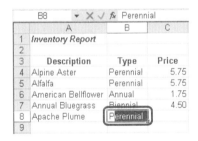

Understanding a Data Form

When you enter information in a worksheet, you'll spend a lot of time moving around the worksheet using the tab and arrow keys on the keyboard. However, if you use a redesigned form to enter information, you'll save both time and hassle. In Excel, you can use the **Data Form** feature to enter data. Excel automatically generates a Data Form based on the field names you assign when you create a list.

Data Form
A dialog box that contains field names from your list range and text boxes you fill in to enter the data.

You can use the Data Form to enter repetitive information one record at a time. You can also use the Data Form to move around in a list and to search for specific data. When you select a list range and open the Data Form, the form displays a field name and text boxes for all fields in the list. If the list already contains data, the data for the currently selected record appears in the text boxes. In a Data Form, you can enter new data in text boxes of a blank record, edit data in existing records (although you cannot change field names), navigate to different records, and search for selected records. You can perform the following functions in the Data Form.

- Click the **New** button to enter a new record.

- Click the **Delete** button to remove an existing record.

- Click the **Restore** button to undo the previous action.

- Click the **Find Prev** button to locate the closest previous record matching the criteria.

- Click the **Find Next** button to locate the closest record matching the criteria.

- Click the **Criteria** button to display the Data Form with all fields blank. Enter the field items you want to find.

- Click the **Close** button to close the Data Form and return to the worksheet.

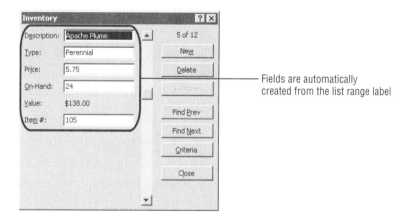

Fields are automatically created from the list range label

Adding Records Using a Data Form

A Data Form provides an optional method of entering information in a list. Once you have entered field names, you can access a Data Form using the Data menu. You don't even need to select the list range first; as long as you open the Data Form when the cursor is in an cell in the list range, Excel will automatically locate the list. As you add new records to the form, Excel updates the list range with the new rows, and automatically enlarges the list range to include them.

Add to a List Using a Data Form

1. Click any cell within the list range. If you have not entered any records for the list yet, click one of the field names.

2. Choose **Data ➢ Form**. The Data Form dialog box opens.

3. Click the **New** button.

4. Type each field entry in the appropriate text box. Click in each field or press the Tab key on the keyboard to move from field to field.

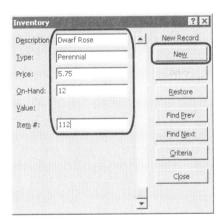

5. Click the **Close** button.

Managing Records Using a Data Form

Criteria
Information on which you perform a search.

You can use a Data Form to display, edit, or delete selected records in a list. To display only selected records in the Data Form, you specify the search **criteria**—the information a record must contain—in the Data Form, and Excel uses that criteria to find and display matching records. Although the Data Form shows only the records that match your criteria, the other records still exist in the list. If more than one record matches your criteria, you can use the Data Form buttons to move through the records, edit them or delete them.

> **TIP** To return to any specific record in Data Form, click the scroll bar located between the field and record buttons.

> **NOTE** By default, the criteria on which Excel searches is not case-sensitive.

Display Selected Records

1. Click anywhere within the list range.

2. Choose **Data ➤ Form**. The Data Form dialog box opens.

3. Click the **Criteria** button.

4. Type the information you want matching records to contain. You can fill in one or more fields.

5. Click **Find Prev** or **Find Next** to advance to a matching record.

6. Repeat step 5 until Excel beeps or until you've finished viewing records.

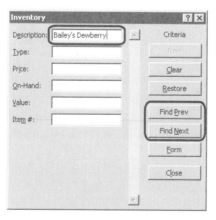

7. Click the **Close** button.

Edit a Record

1. Click anywhere within the list range.

2. Choose **Data** ➤ **Form**. The Data Form dialog box opens.

3. Find a record that requires modification.

4. Click to position the insertion point in the field you want to edit, and then use the Backspace and Delete keys on the keyboard to modify the text.

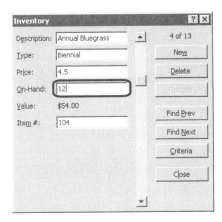

5. Click the **Close** button.

TIP   You can use wildcards to find data in a list quickly. The wildcard "?" stands for any single character, while "*" stands for many characters. R?N might find RAN or RUN while R*N might find RUN, RAN, RUIN, or RATION.

Delete a Record

1. Click anywhere within the list range.

2. Choose **Data** ➤ **Form**. The Data Form dialog box opens.

3. Click the **Criteria** button.

4. Type the information you want matching records to contain. You can fill in one or more fields.

5. Click **Find Prev** or **Find Next** to advance to a matching record.

6. Click the **Delete** button.

7. Click the **OK** button in the warning dialog box.

8. Click the **Close** button.

Sorting Data in a List

Sorting

Alphabetically or numerically organizing a list using one or more fields.

Once you enter records in a list, you can reorganize the information by **sorting** the records. You can sort a list alphabetically or numerically (in ascending or descending order) using one or more fields as the basis for the sort. You can quickly perform a simple sort (sorting a list on one field) using the Standard toolbar, or perform a complex sort (sorting on multiple fields) using the Data menu. A simple sort organizes alphabetically by last name a list that has last names, telephone numbers, and states. Sorting first by state and then by last name is an example of a complex sort. The list will be grouped alphabetically by state and then alphabetically by last name within each state.

Sort Data Quickly

1. Click a field name on which you want to sort.

2. Click the **Sort Ascending** 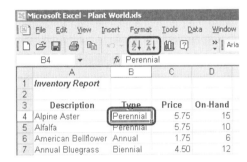 or the **Sort Descending** button on the Standard toolbar. In a list sorted in ascending order, records beginning with a number in the sort field are listed before records beginning with a letter (0-9, A-Z). In a list sorted in descending order, records beginning with a letter in the sort field are listed first (Z-A, 9-0).

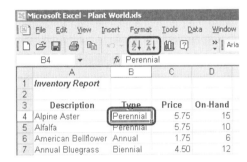

TIP   If you want to sort data in rows instead of in columns, choose Data ➢ Sort, click the Options button, and then click the Sort Left To Right option button in the Sort Options dialog box.

Sort a List Using More Than One Field

1. Click anywhere within the list range.

2. Choose **Data** ➢ **Sort**. The Sort dialog box opens.

3. Click the **Sort By** drop-down arrow ▾, and then select the field on which the sort will be based (the *primary sort field*).

4. Click the **Ascending** or **Descending** option button.

5. Click the first **Then By** drop-down arrow ▾, and then click the **Ascending** or **Descending** option button.

6. If necessary, click the second **Then By** drop-down arrow ▾, and then select the **Ascending** or **Descending** option button.

7. Click the **Header Row** option button to exclude the field names (in the first row) from the sort, or click the **No Header Row** option button to include the field names (in the first row) in the sort.

8. Click the **OK** button.

Displaying Parts of a List with AutoFilter

AutoFilter
A feature that creates a short list of records based on the criteria you selected.

Working with a list that contains numerous records can be cumbersome at best—unless you can narrow your view of the list when necessary. For example, rather than looking through an entire inventory list, you might want to see records that come from one particular distributor. The **AutoFilter** feature creates a list of the items found in each field. You select the items that you want to display in the column (that is, the records that meet certain criteria), which allows you to work with a limited number of records.

> **TIP** The AutoFilter offers a Top 10 command in the drop-down list of every field. Choose Data ➢ Filter ➢ AutoFilter, click a drop-down arrow in a field, and then click Top 10.

Display Specific Records Using AutoFilter

1. Click anywhere within the list range.

2. Choose **Data** ➢ **Filter** ➢ **AutoFilter**. Excel adds a drop-down arrow to each field name.

3. Click the drop-down arrow of the field for which you want to specify search criteria.

4. Select the item that records must match in order to be included in the list.

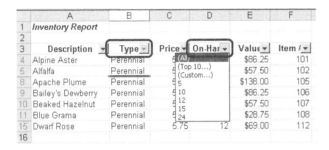

5. Repeat steps 3 and 4, using additional fields as necessary to filter out more records.

6. Choose **Data** ➢ **Form** ➢ **AutoFilter** to turn off AutoFilter and redisplay all records in the list, or click the drop-down arrow of the field and click the **All** button

Creating Complex Searches

There are many times you'll want to search for records that meet multiple criteria. For example, you might want to see the records from a particular supplier that are out of stock. Using the AutoFilter feature and the Custom command, you can create complex searches. You use **logical operators** to measure whether an item in a record qualifies as a match with the selected criteria. You can also use the **logical conditions** AND and OR to join multiple criteria within a single search. The result of any search is either true or false; if a field matches the criteria, the result is true. The OR condition requires that only one criterion be true in order for a record to qualify. The AND condition, requires that both criteria in the statement be true in order for the record to qualify.

Create a Complex Search Using AutoFilter

1. Click anywhere within the list range.

2. Choose **Data** ➢ **Filter** ➢ **AutoFilter**. The Custom AutoFilter dialog box opens.

Logical operators
Arithmetic qualifiers, such as less than, greater than, or equal to that determine if a record matches your criteria.

Logical conditions
Conditions (AND and OR) used to combine multiple search criteria.

3. Click the drop-down arrow next to the first field that you want to include in the search.

4. Click **Custom**. The Custom AutoFilter dialog box opens.

5. Click the **Field** drop-down arrow (on the left) 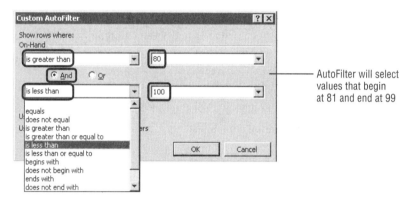, and then select a logical operator.

6. Click the drop-down arrow (on the right), and then select a field choice.

7. Click the **And** or the **Or** option button.

8. Click the drop-down arrow (on the left), and then select a logical operator.

9. Click the drop-down arrow (on the right), and then select a field choice.

AutoFilter will select values that begin at 81 and end at 99

10. Click the **OK** button.

Symbol	Operator
=	Equal to
>	Greater than
>=	Greater than or equal to
<>	Not equal to
<	Less than
<=	Less than or equal to

Entering Data in a List

Entering data in a list—whether you use the Data Form or the worksheet—can be tedious and repetitive. You can enter data using the Pick From List or List

AutoFill feature to make the job easier. **Pick From List** is activated once you have entered at least one record in the list. Pick From List displays previous entries made in the current field in a list format. As you add data to a list, **List AutoFill** considers the preceding cells to determine what formatting and formulas should be extended to the current field.

Enter Data in a List Using Pick From List

1. Right-click the cell in which you want to use, and then click **Pick From List** on the shortcut menu.

2. Click a selection in the list.

3. Press the Enter key or the Tab keys on the keyboard to accept the entry, or press the Esc key to cancel the entry.

Copy Data Formats and Formulas in a List Using List AutoFill

1. Format the data in a list the way you want. For example, you might want to format the fields names in bold and center them.

2. Select the blank cell following the last field name.

3. Type a field name.

4. Click the **Enter** button ☑ on the formula bar, or press the Enter key on the keyboard. Excel formats the new field name with the character-istics you had selected for the previous field names.

Pick From List
A feature that lists previous field entries for you to use to enter information in a field.

List AutoFill
A feature that automatically extends the list's formatting and formulas to adjacent cells.

171

Auditing a Worksheet

In a complex worksheet, it can be difficult to understand the relationships between cells and formulas. Auditing tools enable you to clearly determine these relationships. When **Formula Auditing** is turned on, it uses a series of arrows to show you which cells are part of which formulas.

When you use the auditing tools, **tracer arrows** point out cells that provide data to formulas and the cells that contain formulas that contain formulas that refer to the cells. Excel draws a box around the range of cells that provide data to formulas.

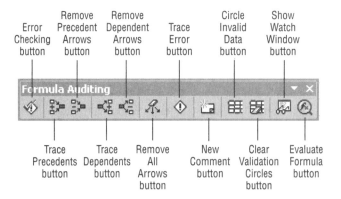

TIP To circle invalid data in a formula, click the Circle Invalid Data button on the Auditing toolbar. To clear the circles, click the Clear Validation Circles button.

Trace Worksheet Relationships

1. Choose **Tools** ➤ **Formula Auditing** ➤ **Show Formula Auditing Toolbar**. The Formula Auditing toolbar opens.

2. To find cells that provide data to a formula, select the cell that contains the formula, and then click the **Trace Precedents** button. An arrow originates in the cell that provides data to the formula and points to the formula

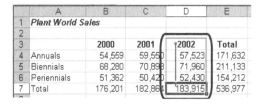

3. To find out which formulas refer to a cell, select the cell, and then click the **Trace Dependents** button ⬚. A bullet appears in the cell and an arrow points to the formula.

4. If a formula displays an error value, such as #DIV/0!, click the cell, and then click the **Trace Error** button ⬚ to locate the problem.

5. To remove arrows, click the **Remove Precedent Arrows** button ⬚, the **Remove Dependent Arrows** button ⬚, or the **Remove All Arrows** button ⬚.

6. Click the **Close** button ⬚ on the Formula Auditing toolbar.

Correcting Formulas

Excel has several tools to help you find and correct problems with formulas. One tool is the Watch window and another is the error checker. The Watch window keeps track of cells and their formulas as you make changes to a worksheet. Excel uses an error check in the same way Microsoft Word uses a grammar checker. The error checker uses certain rules, such as using the wrong argument type, a number stored as text or an empty cell reference, to check for problems in formulas.

Watch Cells and Formulas

1. Select the cells you want to watch.

2. Choose **Tools ➢ Formula Auditing ➢ Show Watch Window**. The Watch window opens.

3. Click the **Add Watch** button ⬚ Add Watch... on the Watch Window toolbar. The Add Watch dialog box opens, display the range of the selected cells.

4. Click the **OK** button. Cell and formula information appears in the Watch window. As you work with these cells and formulas, you can determine their contents at any time.

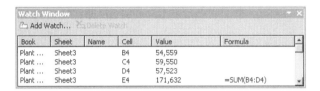

Correct Errors

1. Open the worksheet you want to check for errors.

2. If necessary, choose **Tools ➢ Options**, and then click the **Error Checking** tab, click the **Enable Background Error Checking** check box to select it, click the Rules check boxes in which you want to check to select them, and then click the **OK** button.

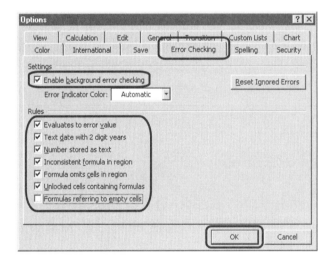

3. Choose **Tools ➢ Error Checking**. The error check scans the worksheet for errors, generating the Error Checker dialog box every time it encounters what is believed to be an error.

4. Choose a button to correct or ignore the problem. The options vary depending on the problem.

10 Sharing Workbook Data

Creating successful workbooks is not always a solitary venture; you may need to share a workbook with others or obtain data from other programs. In Microsoft Excel 2002, you have several choices that you can use to create a joint effort. In many offices, your co-workers (and their computers) are located across the country or the world. They are joined through networks that permit users to share information by opening each other's files and to simultaneously modify data. In addition to sharing workbooks, you can merge information from different workbooks into a single document, and you can link data between or consolidate data from different worksheets and workbooks. By using a variety of techniques, you can link, embed, hyperlink, export, or convert data to create one seamless document that reflects the work of many people.

Exporting and Importing Data

Exporting

A process of copying the current file into another program file.

Importing

A process of copying a file into the current program file.

Importing and exporting information are two sides of the same coin. **Exporting** converts a copy of your open file into the file type of another program. **Importing** copies a file created with the same or another program into your open file. In other words, importing brings information into your open document, while exporting moves information from your open document into another program file. The information becomes part of your open file, just as if you created it in that format, although not all formatting and program-specific information may translate.

There will be times when you will never need to update data that you bring into your Excel worksheet. For these instances, the most expedient way to access the data is to copy and paste it. In other cases, where you will want to update the data that you copy from one program to another, you can convert the data to a format that the other program accepts. If you have text that you want to include on your worksheet, you can import it as a text file.

NOTE Excel can save a file to a format only with an installed converter. If the format you want to save a file in does not appear in the Save As Type list, you'll need to install it by running Setup from the Microsoft Excel 2002 or Microsoft Office XP CD.

Export Excel Data Using Copy and Paste

1. Select the cell or range that you want to copy.

2. Click the **Copy** button ▣ on the Standard toolbar.

3. Open the destination file, or click the program's taskbar button if the program is already open.

4. Position the insertion point where you want the data to be copied.

5. Click the **Paste** button 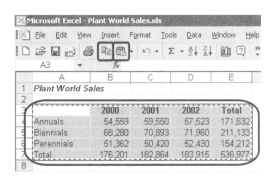 on the Standard toolbar.

Export an Excel File to Another Program Format

1. Open the file from which you want to export data.

2. Choose **File ➢ Save As**. The Save As dialog box opens.

3. Click the **Save As Type** drop-down arrow ☑.

4. Click the file format you want.

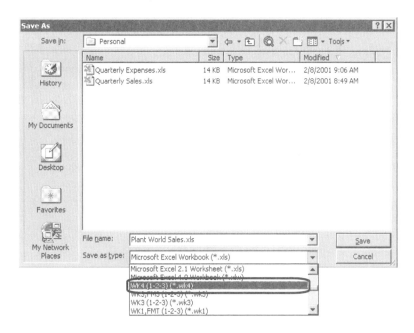

5. Click the **Save** button.

Import a Text File

1. Open the workbook in which you want to insert text data.

2. Choose **Data** ➢ **Import External Data** ➢ **Import Data**. The Select Data Source dialog box opens.

3. Click the **Files Of Type** drop-down arrow ![arrow], and then click **Text Files**.

4. Click the **Look In** drop-down arrow ![arrow], and then select the folder where the text file is located.

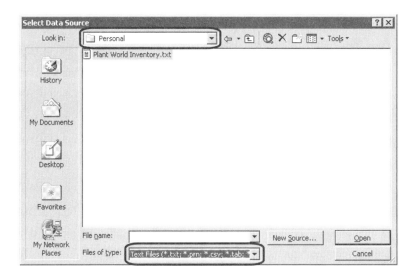

5. Click the text file you want to import.

6. Click the **Open** button.

Linking and Embedding Files

Link
A representative of an original object in a destination file.

Embed
A copy of an object in a destination file.

When you **link** an object, you insert a representation of the object itself into the destination file. The tools of the source program are available, and when you use them to edit the object you've inserted, you are actually editing the source file. Moreover, the destination file reflects the changes that you make to the source file. When you **embed** an object, you place a copy of the object in the destination file. When you select the object, the tools from the source program become available on your worksheet. For example, if you select an Excel chart that you've inserted into a PowerPoint presentation, the Excel menus and toolbars become available. They replace the PowerPoint menus and toolbars, so you can edit the chart if necessary. With embedding, any changes you make to the chart in the presentation do not affect the original file. You cannot update an embedded file.

You can share information that you created using other Office programs, which makes it easy to complete projects such as annual reports or departmental presentations. For example, you can link or embed in a Word document the spreadsheet that you created in an Excel worksheet. Linked data has the advantage of always being accurate because it is automatically updated when you modify the source file.

TIP You can select multiple links by holding down the Ctrl key on the keyboard while you click each link.

Create a Link to Another File

1. Open the source file and any files containing information you want to link.

2. Select the information in the source file, and then click the **Copy** button on the Standard toolbar.

3. Click the insertion point in the destination file.

4. Choose **Edit ➤ Paste Special**. The Paste Special dialog box opens.

5. Click the **Paste Link** button.

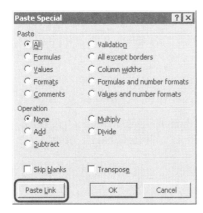

Modify a Link

1. Open the file that contains the link that you want to modify.

2. Choose **Edit ➢ Links**. The Edit Links dialog box opens.

3. Click the link you want to change.

4. Click the **Change Source** button.

5. Select a file from the Change Links dialog box, and then click the **OK** button.

6. Click the **Update Values** button.

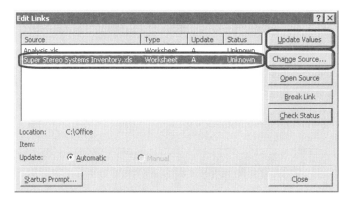

NOTE   You can edit an embedded object only if the program that created it is installed on your computer.

TIP   When you open a workbook that contains links, a warning dialog box opens asking you if you want to update all of the linked information (click the Yes button), or keep the existing information (click the No button).

Embed a New Object

1. Choose **Insert ➢ Object**. The Object dialog box opens.

2. Click the **Create New** tab.

3. Click the object type you want to insert.

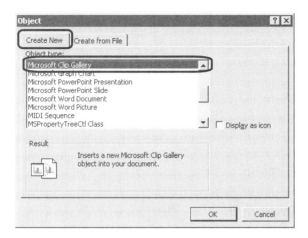

4. Click the **OK** button.

5. Follow the steps necessary to insert the object. The steps will vary depending on the object type.

Embed an Existing Object

1. Choose **Insert ➤ Object**. The Object dialog box opens.

2. Click the **Create From File** tab.

3. Click the **Browse** button, and then locate the file that you want to link.

4. Click the **Link To File** check box to select it.

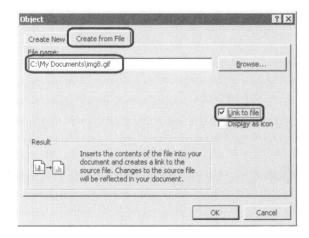

5. Click the **OK** button.

Linking Data

Link
A reference to a cell on another worksheet, or part of a formula.

Source data
The data to be linked.

Destination cell
The cell that is linked to the source data.

Destination range
The range that is linked to the source data.

A **link** can be as simple as a reference to a cell on another worksheet, or it can be part of a formula. Create links instead of entering identical data multiple times; linking data saves time and ensures that your entries are correct. You can link cells between sheets within one workbook or between different workbooks. The cell data to be linked is called the **source data**. The cell or range linked to the source data is called the **destination cell** or **destination range**. If you no longer want to update linked data, you can easily break a link.

Create a Link Between Worksheets

1. Select the destination cell or destination range.

2. Press the = key (an equal sign) on the keyboard.

3. Click the sheet tab that contains the source data.

4. Select the cell or range that contains the source data.

5. Click the **Enter** button ☑ on the formula bar.

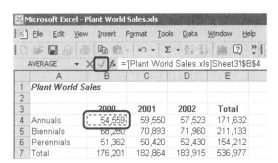

Break a Link

1. Click the cell that contains the linked formula you want to break.

2. Click the **Copy** button 📋 on the Standard toolbar.

3. Choose **Edit ➤ Paste Special**. The Paste Special dialog box opens.

4. Click the **Values** option button.

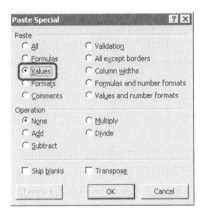

5. Click the **OK** button.

You can arrange worksheet windows to make linking easier by clicking the Window menu, clicking Arrange, and then clicking an option button.

To include a link in a formula, treat the linked cell as one argument in a larger calculation. Enter the formula on the formula bar, and then enter the workbook, worksheet, and cell address of the data that you want to link.

Create a Link Between Workbooks

1. Open the workbooks that contain the data that you want to link.

2. Click the destination cell or destination range.

3. Press the = key (an equal sign) on the keyboard.

4. If the workbook that contains the data you want to link is visible, click anywhere within it to activate it.

5. If necessary, click the sheet tab that contains the source data.

6. Click the **Enter** button ☑ on the formula bar.

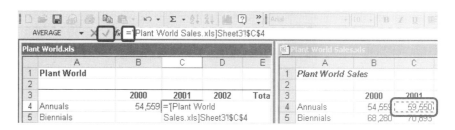

Getting Data from Queries

You can import data into Excel through database and Web queries, analyze the data. You can insert columns within query tables and apply formulas and formatting. When you refresh the data, the formatting and analysis are retained. Excel helps you through the process of bringing data from a Web page to your worksheet. You can create a new Web query as you select the URL and parameters for how you want to import the Web data. Once you save the query, you can run it again at any time.

Get Data from a New Database Query

1. Choose **Data ➢ Import External Data ➢ New Database Query**. The Choose Data Source dialog box opens.

2. Click the **Databases** tab.

3. Click <**New Data Source**>, and then click the **OK** button.

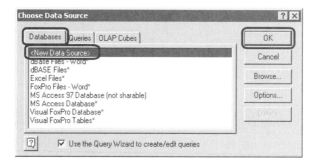

4. In the Create New Data Source dialog box, type a name for your data source.

5. Click the drop-down arrow 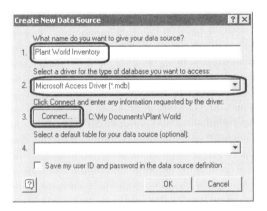, and then select the type of database you want to access.

6. Click the **Connect** button, select or create the database you want to access, and then click the **OK** button.

7. If you want, click the drop-down arrow, and then select the default table for your data source.

8. Click the **OK** button.

9. Click the **OK** button.

TIP To change Web options, choose Tools ➤ Options, click the General tab, and then click the Web Options button. Click the tabs in the Web Options dialog box, change the options you want, and then click the OK button.

Get Data from a New Web Query

1. Choose **Data** ➤ **Import External Data** ➤ **New Web Query**. The New Web Query dialog box opens.

2. Type the address for the Web page that contains the data you want. If necessary, click the **Browse Web** button to help you locate a Web page on the Internet.

3. Click the arrow buttons to select the tables you want.

4. Click the **Import** button.

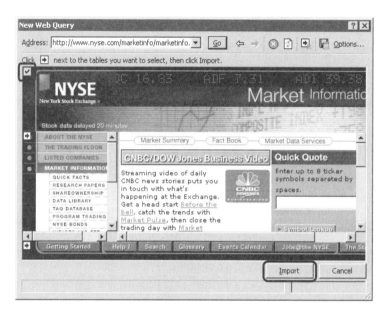

Getting Data from Another Program

The information that you want to analyze may not always exist in an Excel workbook; you might have to retrieve it from another Office program, such as Access. You can easily convert Access table data into Excel worksheet data. Once the data is in Excel, you can use any of Excel's analytical tools (such as PivotTable and AutoFilter) to manipulate this data.

Export an Access Database Table into an Excel Workbook

1. Click the **Start** button 🔳**Start** on the taskbar, point to **Programs**, and then click **Microsoft Access**.

2. Open the database you want, and then click **Tables** on the **Objects** bar.

3. Click the table you want to analyze.

4. Click the **OfficeLinks** button drop-down arrow on the Database toolbar.

5. Click **Analyze It With Microsoft Excel** to save the table as an Excel file, start Excel, and then open the workbook.

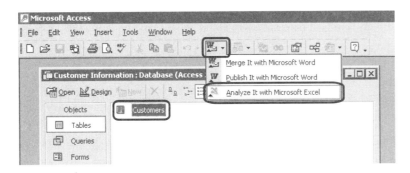

6. Use Excel tools to edit and analyze the data.

Converting Excel Data into Access Data

You can convert your Excel worksheet data into an Access table data using the File Conversion Wizard. This gives you the flexibility of using data created in Excel in Access, where you can take advantage of additional data management and manipulation features.

TIP If you don't see the Convert To MS Access command on the Data menu, install the AccessLinks add-in program from the Web. Choose Help ➢ Office On The Web.

Convert Excel Data to Access Data

1. Select the Excel worksheet data that you want to convert.

2. Choose **Data** ➢ **Convert To MS Access**.

3. Choose to create a new database or to open an existing one.

4. Click the **OK** button. Access starts and creates a new table based on the Excel data in a database.

11 Collaborating with Others

Many projects at work require a group effort. Microsoft Excel 2002 makes it easy for you to communicate with your teammates. Instead of writing on yellow sticky notes and attaching them to a printout, you can insert electronic comments within worksheet cells. You can also track changes within a workbook made by you and others. You can protect your hard work by adding passwords that prevent your co-workers from modifying your workbooks by preventing unauthorized users from opening them.

Sharing Workbooks

When you're working with co-workers in a networked environment, you may want to share the workbooks you've created. You may also want to share the responsibility of entering and maintaining data. **Sharing** means that users can add columns and rows, enter data, and change formatting, while you can review their changes. This type of work arrangement is particularly effective in team situations in which multiple users have joint responsibility for entering the data in one workbook. In cases in which multiple users modify the same cells, Excel can keep track of who made what changes so that you can accept or reject them later.

Enable Workbook Sharing

1. Open the workbook that you want to share.

2. Choose **Tools ➤ Share Workbook**. The Share Workbook dialog box opens.

3. Click the **Editing** tab.

4. Click the **Allow Changes By More Than One User At The Same Time** check box to select it.

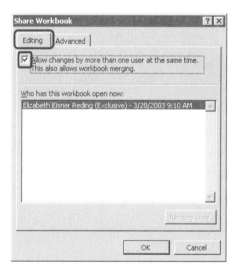

5. Click the **OK** button, and then click the **OK** button again to save your workbook.

Creating and Reading a Cell Comment

Any cell on a worksheet can contain a **comment**—information you might want to share with co-workers or include as a reminder without making it a part of the worksheet. Think of a comment as a sticky note attached to an individual cell. A cell containing a comment displays a red triangle in the upper-right corner of the cell. By default, comments are hidden and display only when you position the mouse pointer over the red triangle. You can choose whether you want to print the comments in a worksheet.

Comment
Text you insert as a note that Excel tags with the initials of the user who enters it. A comment is visible only when you place the mouse pointer over the red triangle.

TIP To add and modify comments using the Reviewing toolbar, right-click any toolbar, click Reviewing to display the toolbar, and then position the mouse pointer over a button to display its function.

Add a Comment

1. Click the cell to which you want to add a comment.

2. Choose **Insert** ➤ **Comment**. A comment box appears.

3. Type the comment in the comment box.

4. Click anywhere outside the comment box when you are finished, or press the Esc key on the keyboard twice to close the comment box.

Read a Comment

1. Position the mouse pointer over a red triangle in a cell to read the comment.

2. Move the mouse pointer off the cell to hide the comment. To show all the comments on the worksheet, choose **View** ➤ **Comments**. The Reviewing toolbar opens with the Show All Comments button selected.

Editing and Deleting a Cell Comment

You can edit, delete, and even format cell comments just as you do other text on a worksheet. For example, you might want to format certain comments to add emphasis, or color-code them by category. If you are working with others online, your readers may want to delete a comment after reading it.

TIP To format a comment quickly, right-click the cell containing the comment, select the comment text, and then click the Bold button, Italic button, Underline button, or an Alignment button on the Formatting toolbar.

Edit a Comment

1. Right-click the cell containing the comment.

2. Click **Edit Comment** on the shortcut menu.

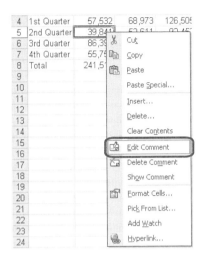

3. Make your changes using common editing tools, such as the Backspace key and Delete key on the keyboard, or with the Formatting toolbar buttons.

4. Press the Esc key on the keyboard twice to close the comment box.

Delete a Comment

1. Right-click the cell containing the comment that you want to delete.

2. Click **Delete Comment** on the shortcut menu.

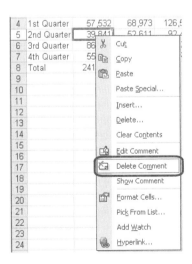

Tracking Changes

Track changes

A feature that lets you see details about changes made to worksheet cells.

As you build and fine-tune a workbook—particularly if you are sharing workbooks with co-workers—you can keep track of all the changes that are made at each stage in the process. The **Track Changes** feature makes it easy to see who made what changes when, and to accept or reject each change. To take full advantage of this feature, turn it on the first time you or a co-worker edits a workbook. Then, when it's time to review the workbook, all the changes will have been recorded. You can review tracked changes in a workbook at any point. A blue border surrounds cells that contain changes, and you can instantly view the changes by moving your mouse pointer over any outlined cell. When you're ready to finalize the workbook, you can review each change, and then either accept or reject it.

Turn On the Track Changes Feature

1. Choose **Tools** ➤ **Track Changes** ➤ **Highlight Changes**. The Highlight Changes dialog box opens.

2. Click the **Track Changes While Editing** check box to select it.

3. Click the **When** check box, the **Who** check box, or the **Where** check box to select them. Click an associated drop-down arrow, and then select the option you want.

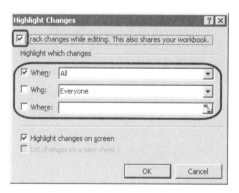

4. Click the **OK** button.

5. Make changes in your worksheet. Column and row indicators for changed cells appear in red. The cell containing the changes has a blue outline.

View Tracked Changes

1. Position the mouse pointer over an edited cell. A box appears listing the user, date, time, the affected cell, and the change you made.

TIP When you or another user applies the Track Changes command to a workbook, the message "[Shared]" appears in the title bar of the workbook to alert you that this feature is active.

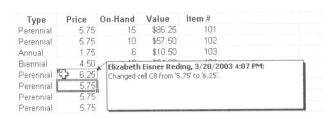

Accept or Reject Tracked Changes

1. Choose **Tools** ➢ **Track Changes** ➢ **Accept Or Reject Changes**. The Select Changes To Accept Or Reject dialog box opens. If necessary, click the **OK** button in the message box.

2. Click the **When** check box to select it, click the **When** drop-down arrow ⏷, and then select a When option.

3. If you want, click the **Who** check box to select it, click the **Who** drop-down arrow ⏷, and then click a Who option.

4. If you want, click the **Where** check box to select it, click the **Collapse** button, and select a range.

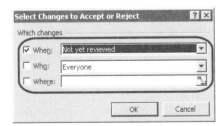

5. To begin reviewing changes, click the **OK** button in the Select Changes To Accept Or Reject dialog box.

6. If necessary, scroll to review all the changes, and then click one of the following buttons.

- **Accept** button—makes the selected change to the worksheet.

- **Reject** button—removes the selected change from the worksheet.

- **Accept All** button—makes all of the changes to the worksheet even if you have not reviewed them.

- **Reject All** button—removes all of the changes to the worksheet even if you have not reviewed them.

7. Click the **Close** button.

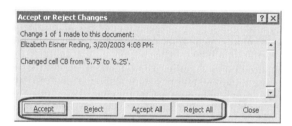

Comparing and Merging Workbooks

For one reason or another, multiple users may maintain identical workbooks. At some point, you'll want to integrate their data into one master workbook, known as the template. First, though, you need to compare the data to identify the differences between the worksheets. Excel can electronically combine the entries, which ensures the integrity of your data.

TIP When merging workbooks, all the workbooks must be identical to the file into which the data is being merged.

Merging Workbook Data

1. Open the workbook that you want to use as the template.

2. Choose **Tools ➤ Compare And Merge Workbooks**. The Select Files to Merge Into Current Workbook dialog box opens.

3. Click the **OK** button to save the workbook, if necessary.

4. Select the files you want merged with the active file.

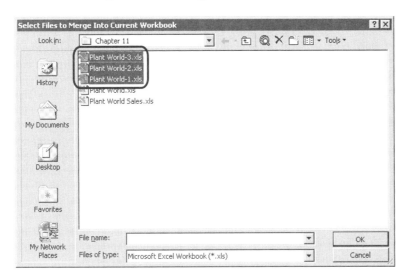

5. Click the **OK** button. Once Excel merges the files, the modifications display in the template workbook.

Protecting Your Data

To preserve all your hard work—particularly if others use your files—you can protect your data by adding a password, which prevents users who do not have the password from removing the data protection you've established. You can select the options you want users to perform; Excel's default is to prevent access unless you select an option. You can protect a worksheet or an entire workbook. In each case, Excel will prompt you to supply a password, and then to re-enter it when you want to work on the file.

> **TIP** You can turn off protection by choosing Tools ➢ Protection ➢ Unprotect Sheet or Unprotect Workbook, enter your password, and then click the OK button.

> **TIP** To share a workbook and prevent track changes from being removed, choose Tools ➢ Protection ➢ Protect and Share Workbook. Click the Sharing With Track Changes check box to select it, enter your password (optional), and then click the OK button.

Protect a Worksheet

1. Choose **Tools** ➤ **Protection** ➤ **Protect Sheet**. The Protect Sheet dialog box opens.

2. If you want, click the **Protect Worksheet And Contents Of Locked Cells** check box to select it.

3. Click the check boxes to select the options you want users to be able to perform in the worksheet.

4. Type a password.

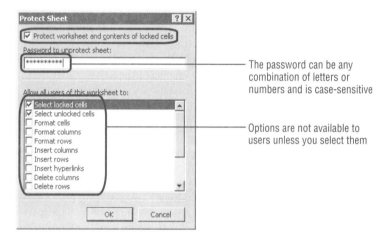

The password can be any combination of letters or numbers and is case-sensitive

Options are not available to users unless you select them

5. Click the **OK** button.

6. Retype the password to confirm it. Keep your password in a safe place. Avoid obvious passwords like your name, your birth date, or the name of a pet.

5. Click the **OK** button.

Protect a Workbook

1. Choose **Tools** ➢ **Protection** ➢ **Protect Workbook**. The Protect Workbook dialog box opens.

2. If you want, click the **Structure** or the **Windows** check boxes to select them.

3. Type a password.

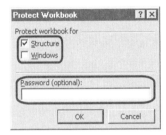

4. Click the **OK** button.

5. Retype the password to confirm it. Keep your password in a safe place. Avoid obvious passwords like your name, your birth date, or the name of a pet.

6. Click the **OK** button.

Sending a Workbook for Review

After you have completed your workbook, you can send it to others for review. The Mail Recipient (for Review) command makes it easy to create and send an e-mail with the workbook attachment and proper follow up settings. When a reviewer receives the e-mail with the attached file and opens the workbook, the reviewing tools are ready to use during the review process. When the reviewers return the file, Excel prompts you to merge the changes with the original workbook. You can use the reviewing tools to accept or reject the changes, or end the review cycle.

Send a Workbook for Review Using E-Mail

1. Open the worksheet you want to send out for review.

2. Choose **File** ➢ **Send To** ➢ **Mail Recipient (Review)**. Your default e-mail program opens, displaying a new e-mail message window.

3. If a message box appears, asking you to save a shared version of the workbook for reviews, click the **Yes** button, and then click the **Save** button to save a shared copy of the file.

4. Click the **To** button, select the contacts to whom you want the message sent, and then click the **OK** button.

5. If you want, type a message for the reviewers.

6. Click the **Send** button 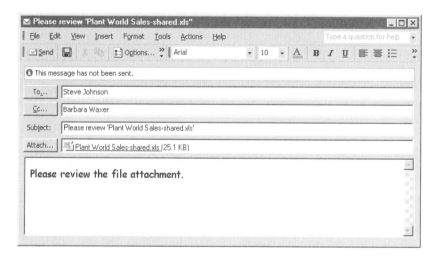 on the toolbar to send the e-mail to reviewers.

7. When the reviewer receives the e-mail, open the file attachment, make changes, and then click the **Reply With Changes** button on the Reviewing toolbar.

8. When you receive the e-mail back with changes, open the file and merge the changes.

9. When you're done, click the **End Review** button on the Reviewing toolbar.

12

Taking Advantage of the Internet

Incorporating hyperlinks within your Microsoft Excel 2002 worksheet adds an element of connectivity to your work. A workbook that accesses the Internet can be a gateway to evolving information. By converting your Excel workbooks to Web pages, you can share your data with others on the Web. A single worksheet can become a window to the world, given Excel's ability to exchange information, analyze data, send files using e-mail, hold meetings, and host Web discussions—and at the same time, maintain all of Excel's functionality. You can add links to other Web sites and obtain data from other Web sources. In addition, Microsoft offers tips and general information through its Microsoft Office Update Web site.

Creating a Web Page

HTML (Hypertext Markup Language)
Coding instructions that are used to create web pages and are interpreted by a browser program.

You can save an existing Excel worksheet as a Web document that others may view in a Web browser. In order to place any document on the Web, you must save it in **HTML (Hypertext Markup Language)** format. HTML is the standard format for posting and viewing data on a Web site. You don't need any HTML knowledge to save an Excel worksheet as a Web page; dialog boxes lead you through all the necessary steps. When you save a worksheet as a Web page, it retains all of its spreadsheet, charting, and PivotTable functionality, and it preserves its formatting properties. This **interactivity** allows others to manipulate your worksheet data on the Web.

Interactivity
The ability for other users to read and make changes to your worksheet data.

You can save an Excel workbook as a Web page in the standard Web page HTML format or the encapsulated MHTML format, known as a **Web archive**. The standard format saves a workbook as a HTML file and creates a folder that stores supporting files, such as graphics and worksheets. The encapsulated format saves all the elements of a workbook, including text and graphics, into a single file in the MHTML format. The MHTML formal is supported by Internet Explorer 4.0 or later. In the Save As dialog box, you use the Save As Type drop-down arrow to select the format you want to use. If you want to automatically update a Web page you created from an Excel workbook, you can use the AutoRepublish option in the Publish dialog. This option republishes the Web page each time you save the workbook.

Web archive
A format that saves all the elements of a Web page into a single file.

Save a Workbook as a Web Page

1. Choose **File ➤ Save As Web Page**. The Save As dialog box opens.

2. Click one of the icons on the **Places** bar to select a location in which to save the Web page.

3. If you want to save the file in another folder, click the **Save In** drop-down arrow ▾, and then select the drive and folder in which you want to save the Web page.

TIP You can save and publish a Web page to an FTP site on the Internet. In the Save As dialog box, click the Save In drop-down arrow, click Add/Modify FTP Locations, fill in the FTP site information, click Add, click the OK button, click the FTP location, and then click the Save button.

4. In the **File Name** box, type the name for the Web page.

5. Click the **Save As Type** drop-down arrow 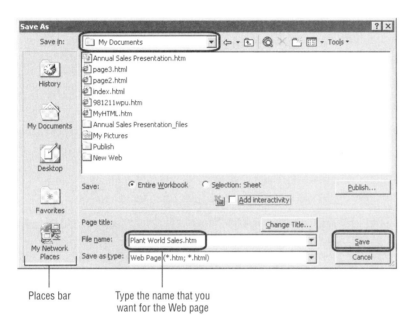, and then click **Web Page** or **Web Archive**.

6. If you want to change the title of your Web page, click the **Change Title** button, type a new title, and then click the **OK** button.

7. Click the **Save** button.

Places bar   Type the name that you
                  want for the Web page

A Web server is a computer on the Internet or an intranet that stores Web pages.

Save and Publish a Worksheet as an Interactive Web Page

1. Select the cell(s) you want to save as a Web page.

2. Choose **File ➤ Save As Web Page**. The Save As dialog box opens.

3. If necessary, click the Selection: *range address* option button to convert the selected range.

4. To add interactivity to your Web document, click the **Add Interactivity** check box.

5. Click one of the icons on the **Places** bar to select a location for the Web page file. If you're connected to a Web server with Office Server Extensions, click the **Web Folders** icon to select a location on the Internet or on your intranet.

6. In the **File Name** box, type the name for the Web page.

7. Click the **Save As Type** drop-down arrow ![arrow], and then click **Web Page** or **Web Archive**.

8. If you want to change the title of your Web page, click the **Change Title** button, type a new title, and then click the **OK** button.

9. Click the **Publish** button. The Publish as Web Page dialog box opens.

10. Click the **Add Interactivity With** drop-down arrow ![arrow], and then click **Spreadsheet** or **PivotTable**.

11. To automatically republish the worksheet when you save, click the **AutoRepublish Every Time This Workbook Is Saved** check box to select it.

12. Click the **Publish** button.

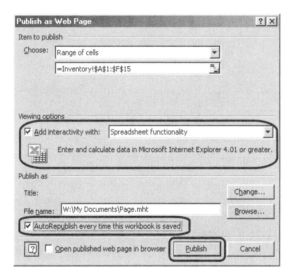

Opening a Workbook as a Web Page

After saving a workbook as a Web page, you can open the Web page as an HTML file in Excel. This allows you to quickly and easily switch from HTML to the standard Excel format and back again without losing any formatting or functionality.

Open a Workbook as a Web Page in Excel

1. Click the **Open** button 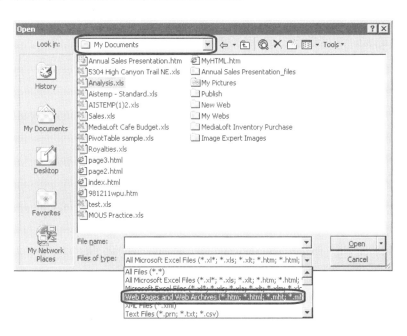 on the Standard toolbar in the Excel window. The Open dialog box opens.

2. Click the **Files Of Type** drop-down arrow, and then click **Web Pages And Web Archives**.

3. Click one of the icons on the **Places** bar for quick access to frequently used folders.

4. If the file is located in another folder, click the **Look In** drop-down arrow, and then select the folder where the file is located.

5. Click the name of the workbook file.

6. Click the **Open** button. The HTML file opens in Excel.

Previewing a Web Page

You can view any Excel worksheet as if it were already on the Web by using the Web page preview feature. By previewing a file you want to post to the Web, you can see if you need to correct errors, change formatting, or add text or data. Just as you should always preview a worksheet before you print it, you should preview a Web page before you post it. Previewing the Web page is similar to using the Print Preview feature before you print a worksheet.

You do not have to be connected to the Internet to preview a worksheet as a Web page.

View the Web Page

1. Open the worksheet you want to view as a Web page.

2. Choose **File ➢ Web Page Preview**. Your default Web browser opens and displays the Web page.

3. Click the sheet tab you want to view.

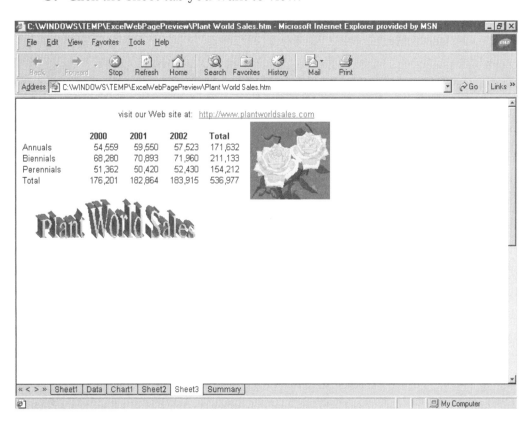

4. Click the **Close** button ☒ to exit your Web browser and return to Excel.

Inserting an Internet Link

Hyperlink

Text or graphic image in a Web page that you can click to jump to another page. Also known as a link.

You can insert links in your worksheet to other Web sites, which is a great way to enhance your worksheet. An Internet link that you embed on a worksheet is called a **hyperlink**—when you click it, you instantly connect to the link's defined address on the Web. The hyperlink appears in the worksheet as blue text. To connect to the Web site, just click the hyperlink once in a cell. To select a cell with a hyperlink, click and hold the cell.

Create a Hyperlink

1. Select the cell where you want the hyperlink to appear.

2. Click the **Insert Hyperlink** button 🔗 on the Standard toolbar. The Insert Hyperlink dialog box opens.

3. In the **Address** box, type the text that you would like the hyperlink to appear as in your worksheet.

4. Click one of the icons on the **Link To** bar for quick access to frequently used files, Web pages, and links.

5. Select the name and location of the file or Web page to which you want to link.

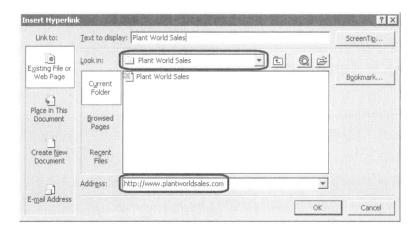

6. Click the **OK** button. The text you selected for the hyperlink appears in the selected cell.

TIP You can create a custom ScreenTip for a hyperlink. Select the hyperlink you want to customize, click the Insert Hyperlink button on the Standard toolbar, click the ScreenTip button, type the ScreenTip text you want, and click the OK button twice.

NOTE Every Web page has a Uniform Resource Locator (URL), a Web address in a form that your browser program can decipher. Each URL identifies where a Web page is located. For example, the URL for Microsoft's Web page is "http://www.microsoft.com/", where "http://" indicates the protocol to use for the Web address, and "www.microsoft.com" shows the computer that stores the Web page.

Jump to a Hyperlink

1. Establish an Internet connection.

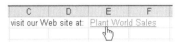

2. Click the hyperlink on your worksheet. Excel opens your Web browser. The browser displays the Web page associated with the hyperlink.

TIP If your hyperlink opens a Web page that is stored on your computer, you do not need to establish an Internet connection.

Remove a Hyperlink

1. Select a cell containing the hyperlink you want to remove.

2. Click the **Insert Hyperlink** button on the Standard toolbar. The Insert Hyperlink dialog box opens.

3. Click the **Remove Link** button. Excel removes the hyperlink, although the text remains in the cell.

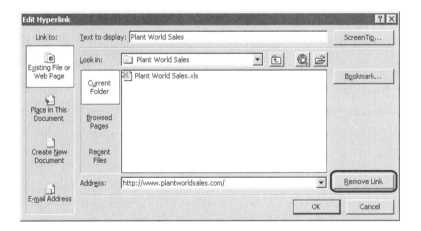

TIP To remove a hyperlink quickly, right-click the hyperlink, and then click Remove Hyperlink.

Getting Data from the Web

Using the Web toolbar, you can gather data on the Web to insert into your worksheet. For example, you might want to include text from a Web site that contains information relevant to your company, audience, or research project. The Web is also a great source of free clip art. Using Microsoft's Clip Gallery Live or other online resources, you can illustrate a worksheet with almost any product, theme, or idea.

 TIP To help you see more information on the screen, you can show only the Web toolbar. To hide the other toolbars, click the Show Only Web Toolbar button on the Web toolbar. Click the button again to display the other toolbars.

Get Data from the Web Using the Web Toolbar

1. Choose **View** ➢ **Toolbars** ➢ **Web**. The Web toolbar opens.

2. Click the **Search The Web** button 🔍 on the Web toolbar. Excel opens your Web browser.

3. Establish an Internet connection.

4. Follow the directions to search for Web sites that contain the data you want.

5. To get text data from a Web page, select the text, click the **Edit** menu, and then click **Copy**. Switch to Excel and then paste the text on your worksheet.

6. To download a file, click the download hyperlink, click the **Save This File To Disk** option button, click the **OK** button, select a location, and then click the **Save** button 💾.

7. When you're done, click the **Close** button ✕.

8. If necessary, disconnect from the Internet.

Get Additional Clips from the Web

1. Choose **Insert** ➤ **Picture** ➤ **Clip Art**. The Insert Clip Art task pane opens.

2. Click the **Clips Online** button, and then Excel opens your Web browser.

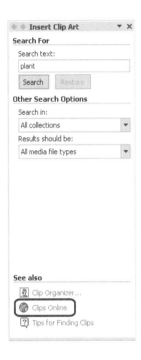

3. Establish an Internet connection.

4. Click a hyperlink on the Clip Gallery Live Web page to access the clip art gallery in which you're interested, and then follow the instructions to download clip art.

5. When you are finished, choose **File** ➤ **Close** in your browser.

6. If necessary, disconnect from the Internet.

Copying a Web Table to a Worksheet

You can copy tabular information from a Web page by pasting or dragging the information into an Excel worksheet. It's an easy way to transfer and manipulate Web-based table data using Excel. Excel simplifies access to table data by making it available to anyone with a Web browser.

TIP You can use the copy and paste function to transfer table data to Excel. In your browser, select the table data you want, choose Edit ➤ Copy, switch to Excel, click the cell where you want to place the table data, and then click the Paste button on the Standard toolbar.

Copy a Web Table to a Worksheet

1. Open your Web browser.

2. In the **Address** bar, type the location of the Web page with the table data you want to copy, and then press the Enter key on the keyboard.

3. Select the table data in the Web page you want to copy.

4. Open the Excel worksheet where you want to paste the table data.

5. Right-click the taskbar, and then click **Tile Windows Vertically**.

6. Drag the selected table data from the Web browser window to the cell on the worksheet where you want to the table data to appear, and then release the mouse button.

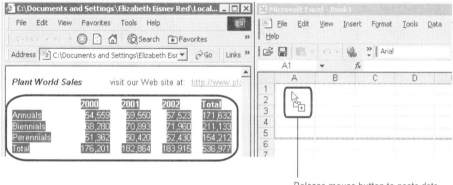

Release mouse button to paste data

Understanding Web Discussions

With the Office Server Extensions installed on a Web server, you can have online discussions in Web page (HTML) files and Office XP documents. A **Web discussion** is an online, interactive conversation that takes place in the Web page or document (also called on-line), or that occurs as a general discussion about the Web page or Office document, which is stored in the discussion pane at the bottom of the page. A Web discussion can occur only through Internet

Web discussion
An online conversation between multiple users that takes place online, within a Web page or document.

Explorer or an Office program. Using the Discussions toolbar, users can insert new comments, edit and reply to existing comments, subscribe to a particular document, and view or hide the Discussion pane.

Having a Web Discussion

Unlike an online meeting, a Web discussion allows multiple users to discuss specific documents. Excel stores the discussions separately from their document counterparts and merges them when you view the results. The documents can be on the Internet, an intranet, or on a network. The advantage to a Web discussion is that Excel preserves the context of your online collaboration in a file that you can view later. You can discuss a worksheet at an online meeting, and then analyze both the worksheet and the discussion it generated.

Select a Web Discussion Server

1. Open the workbook to which you want to add a Web discussion.

2. Choose **Tools** ➢ **Online Collaboration** ➢ **Web Discussions**. If you are selecting a discussion server for the first time, skip to step 5.

3. Click the **Discussions** drop-down arrow ▼ on the Discussions toolbar, and then click **Discussion Options**. The Discussions Options dialog box opens.

4. Click the **Add** button.

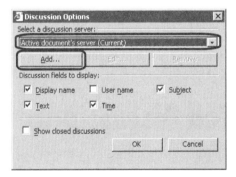

5. Type the name of the discussion server provided by your administrator. The discussion server needs to have Office Server Extensions in order to hold a Web discussion.

6. If your administrator has set up security by using the Secure Sockets Layer (SSL) message protocol, click the **Secure Connection Required (SSL)** check box to select it.

7. Type a name you want to use for the Web discussion.

8. Click the **OK** button.

During a discussion, click the Show/Hide Discussion Pane button on the Discussions toolbar to show or hide the Discussion pane.

To print discussion remarks, start a discussion, click the Discussions button on the Discussions toolbar, click Print Discussions, and then select the print options you want.

Start and Close a Web Discussion

1. Open the workbook for which you want to start a discussion.

2. Choose **Tools ➢ Online Collaboration ➢ Web Discussions**.

3. Click the **Insert Discussion About The Workbook** button on the Discussions toolbar.

4. Type the subject of the discussion.

5. Type your comments.

6. Click the **OK** button.

7. Click the **Close** button Close on the Discussions toolbar.

Reply to a Web Discussion Remark

1. Open the workbook that contains the discussion you want to join.

2. Choose **Tools** ➢ **Online Collaboration** ➢ **Web Discussions**.

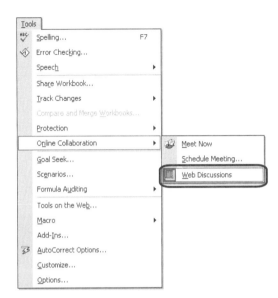

3. Click the **Show A Menu Of Actions** button, and then click the **Reply** button.

4. Type your reply, and then click the **OK** button.

Scheduling and Holding an Online Meeting

In addition sharing information with others online, you can also collaborate with others by using Microsoft NetMeeting to schedule and hold meetings online. When you schedule a meeting online, your attendees can check their calendars, determine scheduling conflicts, and then respond whether they can attend. Holding an online meeting allows people across the country or around the world to meet on short notice without leaving their office or home.

> **TIP** Once you schedule a meeting, you can check to see who will attend. In the Meeting dialog box, click the Attendee Availability tab, and then click the Show Attendee Status option button.

Schedule an Online Meeting

1. Choose **Tools** ➢ **Online Collaboration** ➢ **Schedule Meeting**. The Meeting dialog box opens.

2. Click the **To** button to invite others to join the meeting.

3. Click the **Directory Server** drop-down arrow ▾, select the directory server you want to use, and then enter the organizer's e-mail address, if necessary.

4. Click the **Appointment** tab to determine who will attend the meeting.

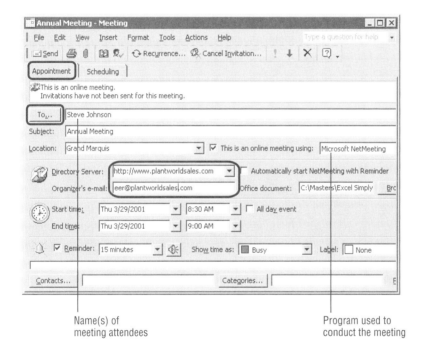

Name(s) of
meeting attendees

Program used to
conduct the meeting

5. Click the **Scheduling** tab to view when attendees are able to meet. Internet users will need to post a calendar to an agreed-upon Web server in order for the host to view your availability.

6. Click the **Send** button ▣ Send on the toolbar.

> **NOTE**   If you receive an online meeting call, click Accept in the Join Meeting dialog box. If you receive an Outlook reminder for the meeting, click Start This NetMeeting (host), or Join This NetMeeting (participant). To receive an Outlook reminder to join a meeting, you need to have accepted the meeting from an e-mail message.

Hold an Online Meeting

1. Open the document you want to share.

2. Choose **Tools** ➢ **Online Collaboration** ➢ **Meet Now**. The Final Someone dialog box opens.

3. If this is your first meeting, select a directory server and enter user information as instructed.

4. If you want, click the **Directory** drop-down arrow 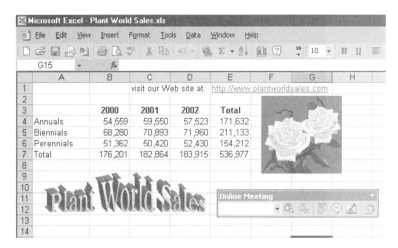, and then select a directory server.

5. If you use MSN, click the **Click Here To Log On To MSN Messenger Service** link, log in to MSN, and select participants.

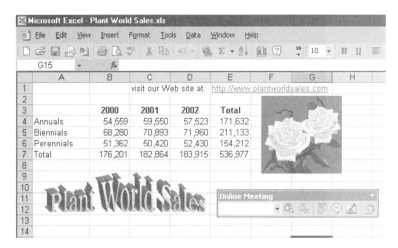

6. Select participants for the meeting, and then click the **Call** button.

Participate in an Online Meeting

Use the buttons on the Online Meeting toolbar to participate in an online meeting.

Button	Description
	Allows the host to invite additional participants to the online meeting
	Allows the host to remove a participant from the online meeting
	Allows participants to edit and control the presentation during the online meeting
	Allows participants to send messages in a Chat session during the online meeting
	Allows participants to draw or type on a Whiteboard during the online meeting
	Allows the host to end the online meeting for the entire group, or a participant to disconnect

Sending Workbooks Using E-Mail

E-mail is a great way to send timely information to friends and business colleagues. You can send a worksheet in the body of an e-mail message or include an entire workbook as a file attachment. You can route a workbook through e-mail, rather than send it to all your recipients at one time. As the workbook is routed through the recipient list, you can track its status. After all of the recipients have reviewed the workbook, it is automatically returned to you.

Send a Worksheet in an E-Mail Message

1. Open the worksheet you want to send.

2. Click the **E-mail** button ⬚ on the Standard toolbar.

3. Click the **To** button or the **Cc** button. Select the contacts to whom you want the message sent, and then click the **OK** button.

4. Click the **Send This Sheet** button on the toolbar.

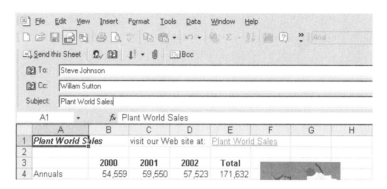

Send a Workbook as an E-Mail Attachment

1. Open the workbook that you want to send as an attachment.

2. Choose **File ➤ Send To ➤ Mail Recipient (As Attachment)**. Your default e-mail program opens, displaying a new e-mail message window.

3. If necessary, click the Profile name for your default mail client, then click the **OK** button.

4. Click the **To** button or the **Cc** button. Select the email recipients, and then click the **OK** button.

5. Type a message.

6. Click the **Send** button on the toolbar.

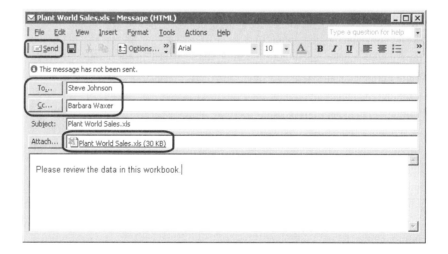

TIP You can change the order in which recipients will receive a routed workbook by changing the order of their names in the list. Select the name of the recipient you want to move, and then click the up arrow or the down arrow.

NOTE You can select a group alias as the recipient. Note that because Excel considers the members of the group alias as one recipient, each will receive one e-mail message. You cannot route a message using a group alias as the recipient.

Route a Workbook in an E-Mail Message

1. Open the workbook that you want to send.

2. Choose **File** ➢ **Send To** ➢ **Routing Recipient**. The Routing Slip dialog box opens.

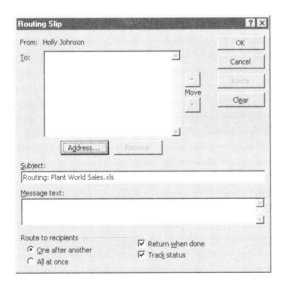

3. Click the **Address** button. The Address Book dialog box opens. Select the contacts to whom you want the message routed, click the **To** button or the **Cc** button, and then click the **OK** button.

4. Type the topic of the message.

5. If you want, type message.

6. Click to select other routing options you want.

7. Click the **Route** button. Excel sends the workbook as an attachment in an e-mail message.

Accessing Office Information on the Web

The Microsoft Office Update Web site maintains current information and assistance for each of its with Office programs. Microsoft constantly updates the site with answers to frequently asked questions, user forums, downloads, and updates. You can also find out about conferences, books, and other products that help you maximize what you can accomplish with your Office programs.

Find Online Office Information

1. Establish an Internet connection.

2. Choose **Help** ➢ **Office On The Web**. Your Web browser opens, displaying the Microsoft Office Web site.

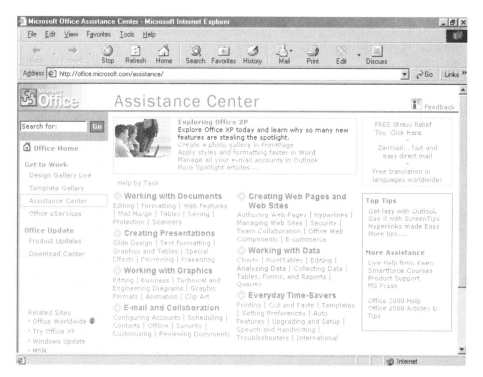

3. Click a hyperlink of interest.

4. When you're done, click the **Close** button to exit the Web browser and return to Excel.

13

Customizing the Way You Work

Microsoft Excel 2002 offers many tools that make the best use of your time. You can customize several settings in the Excel work environment to suit the way you like to work. You can make general changes that affect every workbook, or specific editing options. You can increase your efficiency by customizing the look of the Excel window, the way you execute commands, and the way you create and arrange worksheets in a window. You can maximize your view of the work area, so you spend less time scrolling through a sheet or switching from sheet to sheet, and more time working with data. By creating templates, worksheets that contain formatting and formulas, you can save time and work more efficiently. You can also use speech recognition that lets Excel respond to voice commands.

Changing Options

By taking a few minutes to tailor Excel's work environment, you can maximize your work efficiency. For example, if the folder where you save your workbooks differs from the default folder to which Excel directs you, you can change the default location to where you want to save your workbooks. Or, if you always add two worksheets to your workbooks, you could change the workbook default to open to five worksheets instead of three. You can also change editing options, such as whether the active cell moves after you enter data, and whether to allow drag-and-drop for copying and moving.

Change General Options

1. Choose **Tools** ➤ **Options**. The Options dialog box opens.

2. Click the **General** tab.

3. To turn on a setting in Excel, click the check box for the option that you want to select.

- ◇ Change the number of recently used files listed at the bottom of the File menu by clicking the up or down arrow to set the number of files.

- ◇ Change the default number of sheets in a new workbook by clicking the up or down arrow to set a number.

- ◇ Change the default font by clicking the **Standard Font** drop-down arrow 🔽, and then selecting a new font.

- ◇ Change the default font size by clicking the **Size** drop-down arrow 🔽, and then selecting a new font size.

- ◇ Specify where Excel should automatically look for existing files or where it should save files by entering the location of your default folder.

◆   Click the **User Name** box if you want to edit the name.

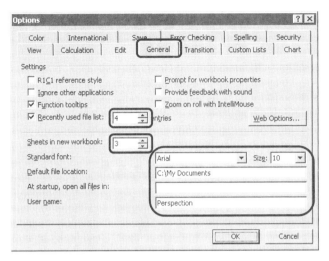

4. Click the **OK** button.

Change Edit Options

1. Choose **Tools** ➢ **Options**. The Options dialog box opens.

2. Click the **Edit** tab.

3. Click the check boxes to change the editing options you want.

◆   Edit directly in a cell.

◆   Use drag-and-drop to copy cells.

◆   Determine the direction the active cell takes once you press the Enter key on the keyboard.

⬥ Determine the number of decimals to the right of the decimal point if using a fixed number format.

⬥ Choose to cut, copy, and sort objects with cells.

⬥ Have Excel prompt you to update links.

⬥ Have Excel provide animated feedback.

⬥ Enable the AutoComplete feature to make data entry easier and more accurate.

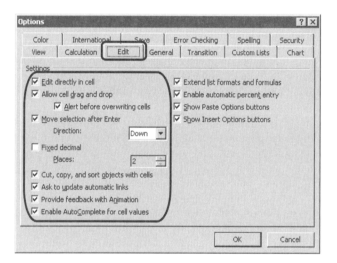

4. Click the **OK** button.

Viewing Multiple Workbooks

You may want to work with more than one workbook at a time. You can arrange multiple workbooks on your desktop in a variety of ways. For example, you might want to compare the data from two fiscal years by viewing the worksheets side-by-side.

NOTE   The bottom of the Window menu lists all open Excel files. The file that contains a check mark is the active file.

TIP   To view different parts of the active workbook in multiple windows, click the Windows Of Active Workbook check box to select it in the Arrange Windows dialog box.

View Multiple Workbooks

1. Open all the workbooks in which you want to work.

2. Choose **Window ➢ Arrange**. The Arrange Windows dialog box opens.

3. Click the arrangement you want for viewing your multiple workbooks.

◆ The **Tiled** option arranges the workbook windows clockwise starting in the top-left position.

◆ The **Horizontal** option arranges the workbook windows one beneath another.

◆ The **Vertical** option arranges the workbook windows side-by-side.

◆ The **Cascade** option arranges the workbook windows one under another.

4. Click the **OK** button.

5. To move from workbook to workbook, click the workbook, or click the workbook button on the taskbar.

6. To return to a single workbook view, click the workbook **Maximize** button ▢ .

Creating a Toolbar

If none of the existing Excel toolbars fits your needs or if you just want to create a toolbar that contains your favorite buttons, you can create a new toolbar. For example, you could add the Page Break button, the Zoom In button, and the Arrow button to a new toolbar. Creating a toolbar that contains the buttons you use most often can dramatically increase your efficiency. Besides creating toolbars, you can change toolbar and menu options to suit your working habits.

Create a Toolbar

1. Choose **View** ➤ **Toolbars** ➤ **Customize**. The Customize dialog box opens.

2. Click the **Toolbars** tab, if necessary.

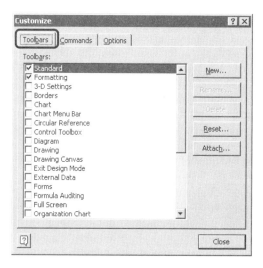

3. Click the **New** button. The New Toolbar dialog box opens.

4. In the **Toolbar Name** box, type a name for the new toolbar.

5. Click the **OK** button. The new toolbar appears as a floating toolbar. The toolbar name may not fit in the title bar until the toolbar contains buttons. The Customize dialog box opens.

6. Click the **Commands** tab.

7. Click a category that contains the command(s) you want to add.

8. Click a command that you want to add to the toolbar.

9. Drag the button to the new toolbar. Make sure that the Customize dialog box does not obscure your view of the new toolbar.

10. Repeat steps 6 through 8 until you add all buttons you want to the new toolbar.

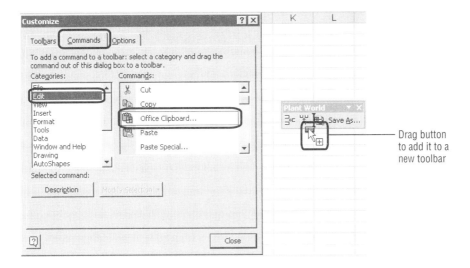

Drag button to add it to a new toolbar

11. Click the **Close** button.

Change Toolbars and Menu Options

1. Choose **View** ➢ **Toolbars** ➢ **Customize**. The Customize dialog box opens.

2. Click the **Options** tab.

3. To maximize space in your work area, click the **Show Standard And Formatting Toolbars On Two Rows** check box to clear it.

4. To turn off personalized menus, click the **Always Show Full Menus** check box to select it.

5. To reset your toolbars and menus, click the **Reset My Usage Data** button.

6. To animate your menus, click the **Menu Animations** drop-down arrow 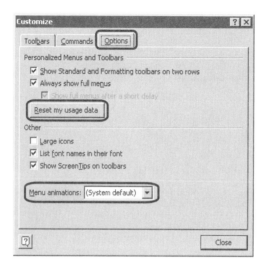, and then select an animation.

7. Click the **Close** button.

Customizing a Toolbar

Excel contains pre-designed toolbars; by default, the Standard and Formatting toolbars appear on the screen at all times. These two toolbars contain buttons for commonly used Excel commands. However, since everyone works differently, you may find that these toolbars display some buttons you never use, while they do not display others you want available on your screen. The Toolbar Options menu customizes these toolbars by displaying buttons you select from the drop-down menu. You can also customize the toolbar by displaying different Excel toolbars, and by adding or deleting different buttons on any toolbar.

Personalize a Toolbar Quickly

1. Click the **Toolbar Options** drop-down arrow on a toolbar.

2. To move a button from **Toolbar Options** to the toolbar, click the toolbar button you want. The toolbar displays the toolbar button.

3. To quickly add or remove a button from a toolbar, point to **Add Or Remove Buttons**, and then click the button you want to add or remove.

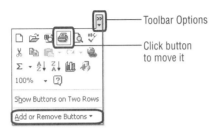

Toolbar Options

Click button
to move it

Delete a Button from a Toolbar

1. Choose **View** ➢ **Toolbars** ➢ **Customize**. The Customize dialog box opens.

2. Click the **Toolbars** tab.

3. Make sure you selected the toolbar from which you want to delete a button.

4. Drag the button that you want to delete off the toolbar.

Drag button
to delete it

5. Click the **Close** button.

> **TIP** To restore a toolbar to its original buttons, choose Tools ➢ Customize, click the Toolbars tab, click the toolbar you want to restore, and then click the Reset button.

> **NOTE** You can assign a button to a macro. Choose Tools ➢ Customize, and then click the Commands tab. Click Macros in the Categories list, click Custom Button in the Commands list, drag the button to a toolbar, click Modify Selection, click Assign Macro, click the macro you want to use, click the OK button, and then click the Close button.

Add a Button to a Toolbar

1. Choose **View** ➢ **Toolbars** ➢ **Customize**. The Customize dialog box opens.

2. Click the **Toolbars** tab, if necessary.

3. Make sure you select the toolbar you want to change.

4. Click the **Commands** tab, if necessary.

5. Click the category that contains the command you want to add.

6. Click the command that you want to add.

7. Drag the button that you want to add to any location on the selected toolbar.

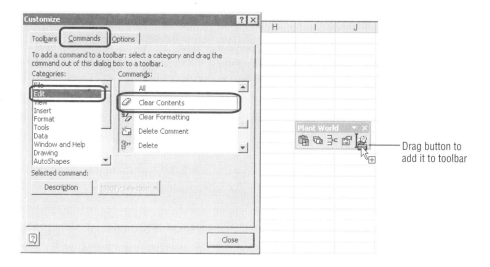

Drag button to add it to toolbar

8. Repeat steps 4 through 6 until you add all the buttons you want.

9. Click the **Close** button.

Creating Groups and Outlines

Outline format
Worksheet data that can be expanded and contracted to show more or less information.

A sales report that displays daily, weekly, and monthly totals in a hierarchical format, such as an outline, helps your reader to sift through and interpret the pertinent information. In **outline format**, a single item can have several topics or levels of information within it. An outline in Excel indicates multiple layers of content by displaying a plus sign (+) on its left side. A minus sign (-) indicates that the item has no contents, is fully expanded, or both.

> **TIP** To clear an outline, select the outline, and then choose Data ➢ Group and Outline ➢ Clear Outline.

> **NOTE** You can ungroup outline data. Select the data group, choose Data ➢ Group and Outline ➢ Ungroup, click the Rows or Columns option button, and then click the OK button.

Create an Outline or Group

1. Organize data in a hierarchical fashion—place summary rows below detail rows and summary columns to the right of detail columns.

2. Select the data that you want to outline.

3. To create an outline, choose **Data ➢ Group And Outline ➢ Auto Outline**.

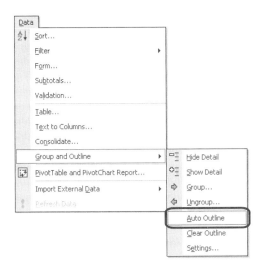

4. To create a group, choose **Data ➢ Group And Outline ➢ Group**. The Group dialog box opens. Click the **Rows or Columns** option button, and then click the **OK** button.

Collapse and Expand an Outline or Group

1. Click a plus sign (+) to expand an outline level; click a minus sign (-) to collapse an outline level. To display specific levels, you can also click 1, 2, and so on.

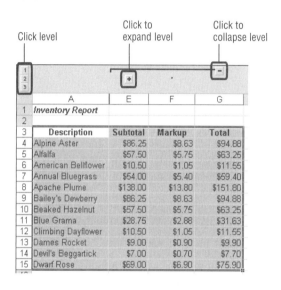

Saving Time with Templates

Template

A workbook with pre-existing text, values, formulas, and formatting that you use to quickly create a new workbook.

Many of the worksheets you create may be similar to those your co-workers also use, such as client invoices. For example, each time you bill a client, you spend time creating an invoice. Wouldn't it be easier if you could open a new workbook that already contained the necessary information, so that all you had to do was fill in the new data as if you were filling in a form? You can create an electronic form by using a template. A **template** is a workbook that can contain formulas, labels, graphics, and formatting. When you start a new workbook based on a template, your new workbook contains all the information from the template; all you have to do is fill in the blanks. Excel contains several built-in templates designed to adapt to almost any business situation.

Create and Save a Workbook Using a Template

1. Choose **File** ➢ **New**. The New Workbook task pane opens.

2. In the **New Workbook** task pane, click **General Templates.** The Templates dialog box opens.

TIP To access templates on the Web, click Templates on My Web sites or Templates on Microsoft.com in the New Workbook task pane.

3. Click the **General** tab or the **Spreadsheet Solutions** tab.

4. Click the template you want to use.

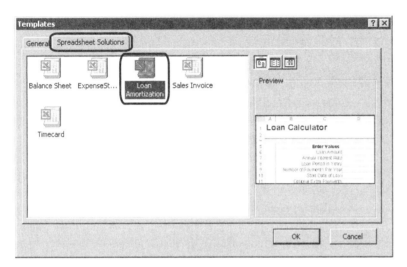

5. Click the **OK** button.

6. Fill in the form with your own information.

7. Click the **Save** button ▣ on the Standard toolbar. The Save As dialog box opens so that you can save the file as a workbook (not a new template).

Template	Description
Balance Sheet	Contains a complex form that lets a user add payments received and those still owed
Expense Statement	Creates a form for submitting business expenses
Loan Amortization	Creates a form for calculating loan payments and interest
Sales Invoice	Creates a form containing customer and product information with unit and extended prices
Timecard	Creates a form into which employee data can be entered

Creating a Template

You can create your own template as easily as you create a worksheet. Just like the default templates that Excel supplies, custom templates can save you time. For example, each month you create an inventory worksheet in which you enter repetitive information; all that changes is the actual data. By creating your own template, you have a custom form that is ready for you to complete each time you take inventory.

TIP As you create a template, enter data in it to make sure that the formulas work correctly. Delete the data before you save it as a template.

NOTE Use a macro to automate repetitive tasks; use a template for fill-in-the-blank data whose format rarely changes.

Create a Template

1. Enter all the necessary information in a new workbook—including formulas, labels, graphics, and formatting.

2. Choose **File** ➢ **Save As**. The Save As dialog box opens.

3. Click the **Save In** drop-down arrow, and then select a location for the template. To have your new template appear in the Spreadsheet Solutions tab of the New dialog box, select the location C:/Program Files/Microsoft Office/Templates/1033.

4. Type a file name that will clearly identify the purpose of the template.

5. Click the **Save As Type** drop-down arrow.

6. Click **Template**.

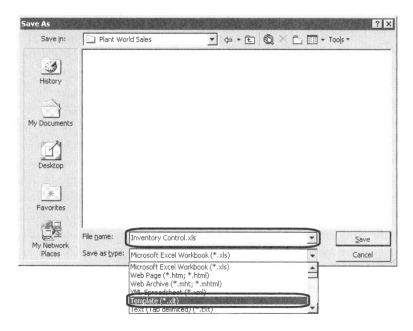

7. Click the **Save** button.

Working with Templates

You may not realize it, but every workbook you create is based on a template. When you start a new workbook without specifying a template, Excel creates a new workbook based on the **default template**, which includes three worksheets and no special formulas, labels, or formatting. When you specify a particular template in the New dialog box, whether it's one supplied by Excel or one that you created yourself, Excel starts a new workbook that contains the formulas, labels, graphics, and formatting contained in that template. You can modify a template by saving it as a template file, instead of saving it as an Excel file.

Default template

The model that determines the contents of a blank workbook.

Open a Template

1. Click the **Open** button 📂 on the Standard toolbar. The Open dialog box opens.

2. Click the **Look In** drop-down arrow 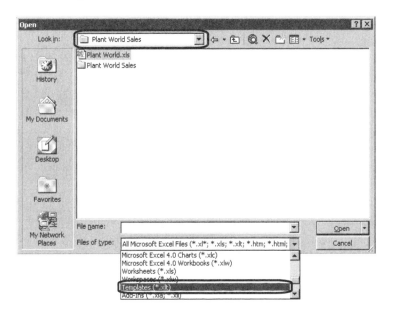, and then select the drive and folder that contain the template you want to open.

3. Click the **Files Of Type** drop-down arrow.

4. Click **Templates**.

5. Click the file name of the template you want open.

6. Click the **Open** button.

Change an Excel Template

1. Click the **Open** button on the Standard toolbar. The Open dialog box opens.

2. Click the **Look In** drop-down arrow, and change the location to C:/Program Files/Microsoft Office/Templates/1033.

3. Click the template you want to modify.

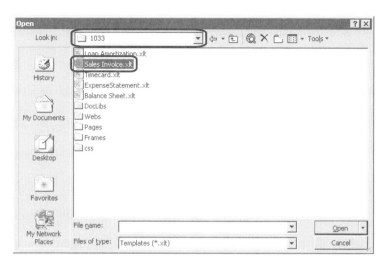

4. Click the **Open** button.

Clicking the New button on the Standard toolbar opens a new workbook based on the default template.

Changing the default template affects all new workbooks you create. Be careful if you decide to make any changes to this template.

5. Make the changes you want. Remember that these changes will affect all new workbooks you create using this template.

6. Click the **Save** button 🖫 on the Standard toolbar.

7. Close the template before using it to create a new workbook.

Controlling Excel with Your Voice

The Office Language toolbar allows you to dictate text directly into your document and also to control buttons, menus and toolbar functions by using the Voice Command option. When you first install an Office XP program, the Language toolbar will appear at the top of your screen. To minimize the toolbar, click the minus sign at the right end of the toolbar. The Language toolbar will dock in the System taskbar at the bottom right of the screen, near the system clock. If you are using English as the default language, the toolbar will be denoted by the letters EN (other languages have appropriate abbreviations as well). To restore the toolbar to the top of the screen, click the icon and select Show the Language toolbar from the pop-up menu.

NOTE You must have a microphone and speakers installed on your computer to use voice and playback features in Excel.

Train Your Computer to Your Voice

Before you can use the Language toolbar for either dictation or voice commands, you must first train your computer to your voice using the Speech Recognition wizard.

1. Click the **Microphone** button on the Language toolbar. The Office Speech Recognition dialog box opens.

2. Click the **Next** button, read the instructions, ensure you are in a quiet environment, and then click the **Next** button again.

3. Read the sentence provided to automatically set the proper volume of the microphone, and then click the **Next** button.

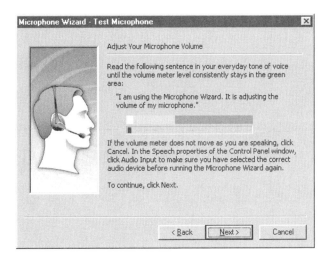

4. Read the text with hard consonants, to help determine whether or not the microphone is positioned too closely to your mouth. Repeat the process, adjusting your microphone as needed until you have a clear, distinct audio playback, and then click the **Next** button.

5. You are reminded to ensure that your environment is suitable for recording again, read the instructions and then click the **Next** button.

6. You are given a series of dialog boxes to read. As you read each paragraph, the words onscreen are highlighted as the computer recognizes them. As each dialog box is completed, the program will automatically move to the next one and the progress meter will update accordingly.

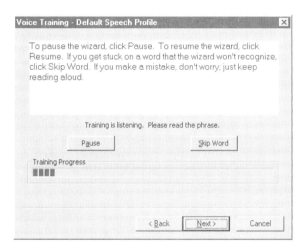

> **TIP**
> It is easier for Excel to recognize complete sentences in context than individual words, so don't pause between each word and wait for the program to display it onscreen.

7. At the end of the training session, your voice profile will be updated and saved automatically.

> **NOTE**
> You are not limited to this one training session. The more that you train, the more accurately Excel will recognize your voice.

Execute Voice Commands

The two modes, Dictation and Voice Command, have been designed to be mutually exclusive of one another. You do not want the word *File* typed, for example, when you are actually trying to open the File menu or, conversely, have the menu open instead of the word *File* being typed when you are in the middle of a sentence. As such, you must manually click on either mode on the Language toolbar to switch between them.

The Voice Command mode allows you to talk your way through any sequence of menus or toolbar commands, simply by reading the appropriate text from them as you would when clicking on them, but letting your words do the work. For example, if you wanted to print the current page of the document you were working on, you would simply say File, Print, Current Page, OK (without saying the commas between the words as written here). You need not worry about remembering every command sequence because as you say each word in the sequence, the corresponding menu or submenu appears onscreen for your reference.

1. Click the **Microphone** button on the Language toolbar. The toolbar expands so that the **Voice Command** button becomes available on the toolbar.

2. Click the **Voice Command** button to shift into that mode.

3. Type the body text of your document normally. When you are ready to issue a command, simply speak the sequence just as you would click through it were you using the menus or toolbars normally (ie: with the mouse, or via keyboard shortcuts, whichever your preference).

Dictate Text

Dictating the text of a letter or other document using Excel's speech recognition functions may be easier for some users than typing, but don't think that it is an entirely hands free operation. For example, you must manually click on the Voice Command button when you want to format anything that has been input, and then click again on Dictation to resume inputting text. Additionally, the Dictation function is not going to be 100% accurate, so you will need to clean up mistakes (such as inputting the word *Noir* when you say or) either when they occur, or subsequently. Finally, although you can say punctuation marks like comma and period to have them accurately reflected in the document, all periods are followed by double spaces (which may not be consistent with the document formatting you wish between sentences) and issues of capitalization remain as well. Nevertheless, it is fun and freeing to be able to get the first draft of any document on paper simply by speaking it.

1. Click the **Microphone** button on the Language toolbar. The toolbar expands so that the **Dictation** button becomes available on the toolbar.

2. Click to position the insertion point inside the document where you want the dictated text to appear and begin speaking normally into your microphone. As you speak, the words will appear on the page.

3. When you have finished dictating your text, click the **Microphone** button again to make the speech recognition functions inactive.

WARNING If you fail to turn off the Language toolbar functions while continuing to work in Excel, distractions in the room like phone calls, even the sound of your keyboard clicking as you type, can introduce errors into your document.

Playing Back Worksheet Data

With Excel, you can have the computer read back data entered on a worksheet. The Text To Speech toolbar gives you options to read back data you select on a worksheet for verification. You can hear the contents of all the cells in a worksheet continuously or each individual cell after you enter data in it. Each cell is selected by row or column and the value or formula is read by the computer. If you hear an error or you're done listening to the data, you can stop the computer from speaking at any time.

NOTE You must have speakers installed on your computer to hear the value of the cells spoken.

NOTE You can double-click the Speech icon in the Control Panel to choose between different computer-generated voices and customize voice settings.

Speak the Value of Cells

1. Choose **Tools** ➢ **Speech** ➢ **Show Text To Speech Toolbar**. The Text To Speech toolbar opens.

2. Select the group of cells you want to hear spoken.

3. Click the **By Rows** button ⊞ or **By Columns** button ⊟ on the Text To Speech toolbar to indicate how you want the computer to read the cells in the worksheet.

4. Click the **Speak Cells** button ⊡ on the Text To Speech toolbar. The computer reads the value of the current cells and moves to the next one.

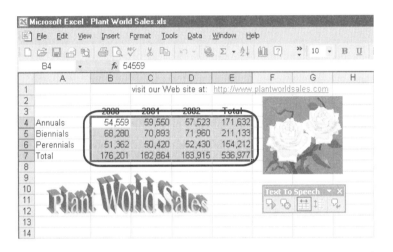

5. When you're done, click the **Stop Speaking** button ⊡ on the Text To Speech toolbar.

> **TIP** To hear the value of a cell spoken after you enter data in the cell, click the Speak On Enter button on the Text To Speech toolbar.

Recognizing Handwriting

Although entering information into an Excel spreadsheet through the keyboard is fast and efficient, you may find that you need to enter information in handwritten form. Excel provides handwriting recognition to help you convert handwriting into text. Before you can insert hand written text into a document, you need to have a third party electronic stylus, handwriting tablet, or mouse attached to your computer. Although you can use the mouse, for best results, you should use a handwriting input device.

When you insert handwritten text into a document that already contains typed text, the handwritten text is converted to typed text, and then inserted in line with the existing text at the point of the cursor. The program recognizes the handwriting when there is enough text for it to do so, when you reach the end of the line, or if you pause for about two seconds. In addition, the converted text will take on the same typeface attributes as the existing text. When you insert text into a blank document, the text is placed at the beginning of the document.

NOTE If the handwriting recognition feature is installed correctly, you'll find the Language toolbar in the upper-right corner of your Excel program window.

Insert Hand Written Text in a Document

When you click the Handwriting button on the Language toolbar and then click the Write Anywhere option, a dialog box similar to the Writing Pad dialog box opens, except there is no writing area within that dialog box. You use this feature just as you would the Writing Pad feature, except that you do your "writing" right on the Excel spreadsheet that is behind the dialog box.

1. Open the spreadsheet you want to insert hand written text.

2. Click the **Handwriting** button on the Language toolbar, and then click **Write Anywhere**.

The Write Anywhere dialog box opens on your screen, and the Text button is selected by default.

3. Move the mouse over a blank area of your spreadsheet, and then write your text. The handwritten words are converted to text on your screen.

Insert Hand Written Text on a Writing Pad

When you click the Handwriting button on the Language toolbar and then click the Writing Pad option, a Writing Pad dialog box opens on your screen. Within that dialog box is another toolbar.

To use the basic features of the Writing Pad, click the Text button, and then move your mouse over the writing area within the dialog box. At that point, the mouse cursor turns into a pen. You then write with that "pen" just as you would write with a physical pen. After recognition, the characters that you write appear in the Excel spreadsheet that is open behind the dialog box. You use other buttons with the dialog box to manipulate the position of the cursor in the Excel spreadsheet itself.

1. Open the spreadsheet you want to insert hand written text.

2. Click the **Handwriting** button on the Language toolbar, and then click **Writing Pad**. The Writing Pad dialog box opens on your screen.

3. Move the mouse cursor over the writing area of the Writing Pad dialog box, write your text. The new text is inserted into the document.

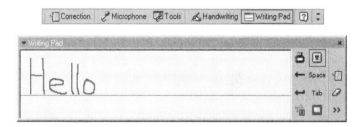

Repairing Office Programs

Despite your best efforts or computer hardware, there will be times when an Office program stops working for no apparent reason. All the Office programs are self-repairing, which means that Office checks if essential files are missing or corrupt as a program opens and fixes the files as needed. You may never even realize there was a problem. Other times, Office starts fine but might have another problem, such as a corrupted font file or a missing template. These kinds of problems used to take hours to identify and fix. Now Office does the work for you with **Detect and Repair**, which locates, diagnoses, and fixes any errors in the program itself. If you need to add or remove features, restore the Office installation, or remove Office entirely, you can use Office Setup's maintenance feature.

Detect and Repair
A feature that allows Office to fix missing or corrupted program files.

Detect and Repair Problems

1. Choose **Help ➣ Detect And Repair**. The Detect and Repair dialog box opens.

2. Click the **Start** button. Insert the Office CD in your CD-ROM drive.

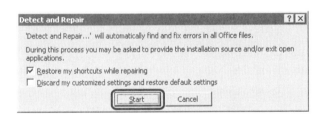

3. If necessary, click **Repair Office**, and then click the **Reinstall Office** or **Repair Errors In Your Office Installation** option button.

4. Click the **Finish** button.

Perform Maintenance on Office Programs

1. In Windows Explorer, double-click the Setup icon on the Office CD.

2. Click one of the following maintenance buttons.

   ◇ **Add Or Remove Features** to determine which and when features are installed or removed.

   ◇ **Repair Office** to repair or reinstall Office.

245

◇ **Uninstall Office** to uninstall Office.

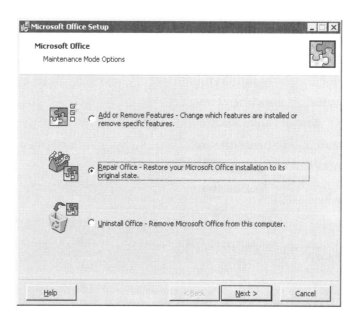

3. Follow the wizard instructions to complete the maintenance.

Glossary

Absolute cell reference
An address that locks the cell reference to cells in the formula.

Active sheet
The sheet on which you are currently working.

Argument
The cell references or values in a formula that contribute to the result. Each function uses function-specific arguments, which may include numeric values, text values, cell references, ranges of cells, and so on.

Attributes
Effects that change the appearance of characters.

AutoCalculate
A feature that automatically displays the sum, average, maximum, minimum, or count of the selected values on the status bar, but does not print.

AutoComplete
A feature that finishes entering your text entries based on the entries you previously entered in a column. AutoComplete does not work with numbers, dates, or times.

AutoCorrect
A feature that automatically detects and corrects misspelled words, grammatical errors, and incorrect capitalization, or completes specific terms.

AutoFill
A feature that fills in data based on entries in adjacent cells.

AutoFilter
A feature that creates a short list of records based on the criteria you selected.

AutoFit
A feature that automatically resizes a column or row to the width/height of its largest entry.

AutoFormat
Pre-designed format that you can apply to data ranges, and include numeric formats and font attributes.

Automatic page breaks
A control that Excel automatically inserts to begin a new page.

AutoShapes
Preset objects, such as arrows, common shapes, banners, circles, or callouts.

Chart
A visual representation of selected worksheet data.

Chart Axis
The vertical or horizontal grid on which data is plotted.

Chart Objects
Individual items within a chart (such as a title or legend) that you can select and modify.

Chart Options
Augmentations and enhancements that you can add to a chart.

Chart Text
Objects containing text, such as data labels and titles.

Chart Title
Text you can insert to clarify the purpose of the chart.

Chart Wizard
A series of dialog boxes that require your input in order to create a chart.

Clips
Artwork you can insert from the Clip Gallery.

Comment
Text you insert as a note that Excel tags with the initials of the user who enters it. A comment is visible only when you place the mouse pointer over the red triangle.

Conditional formatting
Formatting that appears depending on a cell's value or formula.

Contiguous
Adjacent, or touching, cells.

Copy
A command that creates a duplicate of selected cells.

Criteria
Information on which you perform a search.

Data Form
A dialog box that contains field names from your list range and text boxes you fill in to enter the data.

Data Point
A single value in a data series.

Data Series
A collection of associated data that Excel uses to plot any chart type.

Default template
The model that determines the contents of a blank workbook.

Destination cell
The cell that is linked to the source data.

Destination range
The range that is linked to the source data.

Detect and Repair
A feature that allows Office to fix missing or corrupted program files.

Diagram
A collection of shapes that illustrates conceptual material.

Dialog box
A window that displays onscreen that you use to enter or select information.

Drag-and-drop
A technique for moving or copying data.

Edit mode
Status bar state indicating that you can edit the contents of a cell.

Embed
A copy of an object in a destination file.

Exporting
A process of copying the current file into another program file.

Fill handle
A tool that copies cell data or fills in a series of cells. When you select a cell, the fill handle is a small black box. When you point to the fill handle, it changes to a black plus sign.

Font
A collection of characters (letters and numbers) that have the same design qualities, such as size, typeface, and spacing.

Format
Changing the appearance of labels and values in a worksheet.

Formula
A series of values, cell references, and mathematical operators that results in a calculation.

Formula Auditing
A feature that helps you determine relationships between cells.

Freeform
A drawing with irregular curves and straight lines or a polygon that you create.

Freeze
A feature that temporarily fixes column or row headings so they are always visible on the screen.

Functions
Built-in formulas that make it easy to create complex calculations that involve one or more values, performing an operation, and returning one or more values.

Graphic images
Artwork in an electronic file that you can insert from an external source.

Gridlines
Horizontal or vertical lines of a specified width and interval that aid in a chart's readability.

Handles
Small black squares that surround the chart when it is selected.

Header buttons
Buttons at the top of each column and to the left of each row that you can click to select an entire column or row.

Horizontal alignment
Aligning cell contents relative to the left and right edge of the cell.

Horizontal or vertical page breaks
Controls that let you determine where a new page will begin.

HTML (Hypertext Markup Language)
Coding instructions that are used to create web pages and are interpreted by a browser program.

Hyperlink
Text or graphic image in a Web page that you can click to jump to another page. Also known as a link.

Importing
A process of copying a file into the current program file.

Insert Function
A feature that organizes Excel's functions and makes it easy to create a complex calculation.

Interactivity
The ability for other users to read and make changes to your worksheet data.

Keyword
Text you enter in response to a search request, which Excel uses to search for files or information.

Label
Cell text used in titles and column or row headings, and not included in calculations.

Label range
A group of row and column labels that you want to use in your formulas.

Legend
An identifier that matches colors or patterns in the chart with data.

Lines
Straight or curved lines (arcs) that connect two points.

Link (to an object)
A representative of an original object in a destination file.

Link (to data)
A reference to a cell on another worksheet, or part of a formula.

List
A collection of related records in an Excel worksheet.

List AutoFill
A feature that automatically extends the list's formatting and formulas to adjacent cells.

Logical conditions
Conditions (AND and OR) used to combine multiple search criteria.

Logical operators
Arithmetic qualifiers, such as less than, greater than, or equal to that determine if a record matches your criteria.

Margins
The blank area at the top, bottom, left, and right of the page.

Marquee
An outline surrounding selected cells.

Motion clips
An animated picture—also known as an animated GIF—frequently used in Web pages.

New page break
A control that inserts a page break below and to the right of the selected cell.

Noncontiguous
Cells that are not adjacent, or touching.

Numeric formats
Displaying values in different formats, such as changing the number of decimal places or whether currency symbols appear.

Office Assistant
An animated Help feature that displays helpful tips while you are working in Excel.

Office Clipboard
A temporary area that holds up to 24 pieces of copied information and is available from within any Office program.

Organization chart
A graphic map that uses boxes to illustrate the hierarchy within an organization.

Orientation
The appearance of cell text, which can be level or tilted or rotated horizontally up or down.

Outline format
Worksheet data that can be expanded and contracted to show more or less information.

Page break preview
A feature that lets you move page breaks as you view your work.

Page orientation
Determines how the worksheet data is arranged on the page when you print it—vertically or horizontally.

Paint
The process of applying the attributes of a cell's contents to one or more other cells.

Panes
Individual window sections.

Paper size
The physical dimensions of the paper on which data is printed.

Paste
A command that places the duplicated cells in another location.

Pick From List
A feature that lists previous field entries for you to use to enter information in a field.

Point
The unit of height measure for a character, approximately 1/72 of an inch.

Print area
The specific range you want to print.

Print preview
A miniature display of the any portion of the worksheet that shows how the worksheet will look when it is printed.

Print scaling
Resizes text and graphics to fit a specific paper size.

Print titles
Column and row titles that Excel prints on each page.

Range
One or more cells that you've selected.

Range reference
The cell address that displays in the name box.

Relative addressing
The automatic adjustment of cell references that results when a formula is moved or copied.

Select
Click a cell to make it active.

Selection handles
Small circles that appear on the edges of an object when it is selected.

Sharing
The process of making a workbook available for modification by other users.

Smart tag
A button that helps you control the results of certain actions, such as insert financial information, copy and paste, or automatic text correction.

Sorting
Alphabetically or numerically organizing a list using one or more fields.

Source data
The data to be linked.

Spreadsheet program
A type of software you can use to enter, evaluate, manipulate, and communicate quantitative information.

Style
Predefined collections of formats, including fonts, font sizes, and attributes, that you can apply to cells and their contents.

Task pane
An expanded display area to the right of the main window that displays groups of related commands and wizards.

Template
A workbook with pre-existing text, values, formulas, and formatting that you use to quickly create a new workbook.

Tracer arrows
An auditing tool that points out relationships between cells.

Track changes
A feature that lets you see details about changes made to worksheet cells.

Typeface
A specifically named design given to letters and numbers.

Value
The number you enter in a cell that is in calculations.

Vertical alignment

Aligning cell contents relative to the top and bottom edge of the cell.

Web archive

A format that saves all the elements of a Web page into a single file.

Web discussion

An online conversation between multiple users that takes place online, within a Web page or document.

Windows Clipboard

A temporary area that holds the most recently copied piece of information from a Windows program.

Wizard

A utility that leads you through steps to produce a product or accomplish a task.

WordArt

A feature that lets you enhance text by stretching, skewing, and applying special effects to it.

Workbook

The file you create that contains one or more worksheets.

Worksheet

A page from a workbook that contains lines and grids.

Index

SPECIAL CHARACTERS

NUMBERS

A